B
WILSON

Rogers, James T.
Woodrow Wilson.

$19.95   11BT01747

DATE			

WOODROW WILSON

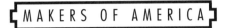
MAKERS OF AMERICA

WOODROW WILSON

Visionary for Peace

JAMES T. ROGERS

Facts On File, Inc.

Woodrow Wilson: Visionary for Peace

Copyright © 1997 by James T. Rogers

Facts On File, Inc.
11 Penn Plaza
New York NY 10001

Library of Congress Cataloging-in-Publication Data

Rogers, James T.
    Woodrow Wilson : visionary for peace / James T. Rogers.
    p. cm.—(Makers of America series)
Includes bibliographical references.
    ISBN 0–8160–3396–X
    1. Wilson, Woodrow, 1856–1924—Juvenile literature.
    2. Presidents—United States—Biography—Juvenile literature.
    3. Historians—United States—Biography—Juvenile literature.
    4. Princeton University—Presidents—Biography—Juvenile literature.
    5. Governors—New Jersey—Biography—Juvenile literature.
    I. Title. II. Series: Makers of America (Facts on File, Inc.)
E767.R58 1997
973.91'3'092
[B]—dc20   96-34549

Text design by Catherine Rincon
Cover design by Matt Galemmo

This book is printed on acid-free paper.

Printed in the United States of America

MP FOF 10 9 8 7 6 5 4 3 2 1

CONTENTS

INTRODUCTION

The Crusade

The president was stumping the country to rouse support for a bold new idea: the United States, historically proud of its independence in world affairs, should surrender some of that independence by joining the new League of Nations—a world parliament aimed at settling disputes by discussion instead of war. No president before him had campaigned across the nation with quite such intensity and single-mindedness. Through Columbus, Indianapolis, St. Louis, Des Moines and many other cities the special presidential train rolled. At each stop, huge crowds turned out to see and cheer the slender figure standing in an open car, doffing his top hat repeatedly in response to the cheers. Then he would go to a large hall, usually hot and without amplifiers so that he had to strain to make himself heard by people in the distant seats, and talk without text or notes for about an hour. He made 40 speeches in 22 days.The crowds responded enthusiastically, and it seemed as though he was winning his crusade.

That president was Woodrow Wilson, a man with a long record of advancing bold new ideas—as a college teacher, president of Princeton University, governor of New Jersey and finally as president of the United States for eight years (1913–21). It was he who almost single-handedly engineered the creation of the League of Nations as part of the treaty ending World War I (1914–18). The work entailed another new venture on his part: Wilson went twice to Paris to participate for extended periods in the drafting of the treaty—the first time an American president had gone so far away or left the country for such a long time.

Returning in 1919, Wilson found that a substantial number of senators wanted changes in the treaty. Without the approval of the Senate, the United States could not sign the treaty or join the League of Nations. He believed that if he carried his message to the public, the response would overcome the opposition in the Senate. That was why he began his national tour, over the objections of his wife and his doctor, who thought he was worn out from his exertions in Paris and in frail health from an attack of flu. "I cannot put my personal safety, my health, in the balance against my duty," he said. "I must go."[1]

But by the time the special train reached Montana, Wilson was beginning to suffer severe headaches. They grew worse as he reached the West Coast. When the tour reached Pueblo, Colorado, on September 25, he was in unrelenting pain. Edmund W. Starling, the Secret Service man who usually accompanied Wilson in his public appearances, became gravely concerned when the president stumbled on a step as he entered the auditorium where he was to speak. Starling's concern grew as he found that he had to help Wilson get up onto the platform and that Wilson allowed him to help—something that he had always refused to allow previously. Starling was not alone in worrying. Newspaper reporters noted that Wilson showed signs of distress during his speech at Pueblo.

That night, on the train, the splitting headache kept the president from sleeping. In the morning, preparing for an appearance in Wichita, Kansas, he found that he could not go on. The tracks were cleared so that the train could speed back to Washington, D.C. At Union Station, the president was able to walk to his car. Wilson's condition seemed to improve over the next few days, but on October 2 he suffered a massive stroke that paralyzed his left arm and leg and for a time impaired his mental ability.

Without its leader, the battle for the treaty was lost. But ultimately, the bold idea was not. "I can predict with absolute certainty," he had said, "that within another generation there will be another World War if the nations of the world do not concert the method by which to prevent it."[2] There was—World War II, fought from 1939 to 1945 and involving many of the same nations that participated in the carnage of World War I. This time, however, the United States joined the world parliament established after the war to preserve peace: the United Nations. The boldest of Wilson's many bold ideas had succeeded at last.

Notes

1. Arthur S. Link, *Woodrow Wilson: A Brief Biography* (Cleveland: The World Publishing Company, 1963), p. 164.

2. Josephus Daniels, *The Wilson Era, Years of War and After—1917–1923* (Chapel Hill, N.C.: The University of North Carolina Press, 1945), p. 480.

WOODROW WILSON

1

THE YOUNG WILSON
(1856–1885)

H e started life as Thomas Woodrow Wilson—having been named for one of his grandfathers, the Reverend Thomas Woodrow—and was called Tommy throughout his childhood. Grandfather Woodrow was a Presbyterian minister who had come to the United States from Scotland in 1836. Tommy's father, the Reverend Joseph Ruggles Wilson, was also a Presbyterian minister, and Tommy was born three days after the Christmas of 1856 in the Presbyterian manse at Staunton (pronounced Stanton), Virginia. His mother had been christened Janet Woodrow but was known to her family as Jeanie and to close friends as Jessie. Tommy was her third child, after Marion and Annie; her fourth and last child was Joseph R. Wilson, born in 1866.

Tommy spent his entire childhood in the South as his father moved from church to church—to Augusta in Georgia, Columbia in South Carolina and Wilmington in North Carolina. In later life, Wilson remarked that "the only place in the country, the only place in the world, where nothing has to be explained to me is the South."[1] As a young boy, Wilson was just old enough to be aware of events in the Civil War. "My earliest recollection," he said in 1909, "is of standing at my father's gateway in Augusta, Georgia, when I was four years old, and hearing someone pass and say that Mr. Lincoln was elected and there was to be war."[2] War there was, and it touched the

Woodrow Wilson's birthplace in Staunton, Virginia, was the Presbyterian manse in 1856, when Wilson was born in the house. His father, the Reverend Joseph Ruggles Wilson, was minister of the Presbyterian church in Staunton. The house is now owned by the Woodrow Wilson Birthplace Foundation, which keeps it open for visitors. (Library of Congress)

family in various ways. Dr. Wilson's church served as a hospital for wounded Confederate soldiers, and Union soldiers taken prisoner were held behind a fence in the churchyard. Woodrow Wilson's sympathies lay with the South and the Confederacy ever afterward, athough he never dwelled on the point.

Until he was 10 years old, Tommy's education was at home. Dr. Wilson had a passion for the precise use of words, and he constantly drilled his son on saying exactly what he meant. When Tommy was old enough to write, his father would have him write a paper on what they had discussed or seen. If the wording was vague, Dr. Wilson would ask what the boy had intended to say. When he heard the answer, he would respond: "Well, you did not say it, so suppose you try again and see if you can say exactly what you mean, and if not we'll have another go at it."[3] The drill usually sent Tommy to the dictionary, sharpening his sense of the exact meaning of the words in question. Dr. Wilson also stressed to the boy the importance of being able to think on his feet and to talk without mumbling or faltering. The future president's reputation as a skilled writer and outstanding public speaker rested on these early drills by his father.

But life was not all drills; Tommy also had plenty of time to play. When he was small, he and his cousin Jessie Bones played at being Indians, staining their faces with pokeberry juice, wearing feathered headdresses and stalking through the woods with tomahawks. As a teenager, Tommy developed an interest in baseball and ships. He was already beginning to picture himself as a leader. He organized several of his friends into the Lightfoot Club, which was both a baseball team and a discussion group with precise rules written by Tommy. Pursuing his interest in ships alone, he became the imaginary Vice Admiral Thomas W. Wilson. Buttressing that role, he familiarized himself with every type of sailing ship and made remarkably accurate drawings of them. In his teens, Tommy wrote rules and regulations for the imaginary Royal United Kingdom Yacht Club, of which Lord Thomas W. Wilson, duke of Carlton and admiral of the Royal Navy, was commodore.

One day Jessie Bones came across her cousin as he was looking at a painting. She asked who was the old man in it. He replied: "That is the greatest statesman who ever lived, Gladstone, and when I grow to be a man I mean to be a great statesman too."[4] (William E. Gladstone was prime minister of Great Britain four times between 1868 and 1894.)

It was activities and ambitions like these that prompted a family servant to describe Tommy as "an old young man who tried to explain the reason of things."[5] In later years, Bliss Perry, who had been one of Wilson's colleagues on the Princeton faculty, said of him:

> When I first knew him, he was only thirty-six, but there was little that was youthful in him except high spirits, energy, and self-confidence. He had never, I suspect, been a boy of normal boyish irresponsibility. His father, who often paid long visits to Princeton and was a whimsical, forceful person, had been "Tommy's" real comrade and had molded his mind and behavior. The son was a true child of a manse where religion, wit, and political theorizing went hand in hand. Both father and son were idealists, phrase-lovers, and critics.[6]

In the autumn of 1873, three months before his 17th birthday, Wilson left home for the first time to enroll as a freshman at Davidson College, a Presbyterian institution in North Carolina. The family's expectation was that he would study to become a Presbyterian minister, like his father and his grandfather. At Davidson he joined a debating society, played on the freshman baseball team and studied earnestly. His marks were fairly good, the lowest one being 74 in mathematics in the first semester—a grade that he raised to 88 in the second semester. But in the spring of 1874, he had a prolonged illness that he called a cold, accompanied by nervous indigestion. He had many periods of respiratory and digestive distress during his life. Dr. Edwin A. Weinstein, a physician who studied Wilson's medical records, believed most of those illnesses were psychosomatic—caused by mental stress. In this case, Weinstein said, Wilson "simply was not emotionally prepared to leave home."[7] Anyway, for what the family called reasons of health, Wilson did not return to Davidson for his sophomore year, instead spending the year at home with his family in Wilmington.

The following year, he started over again, enrolling as a freshman at what was then called the College of New Jersey. (The institution changed its name to Princeton University in 1896, the 150th anniversary of its founding, and Wilson—by then a professor at the university—gave the sesquicentennial address.) Wilson became a prominent member of the class of 1879, counted many of its members as close friends throughout his life and participated enthusiastically in its alumni activities following graduation.

His academic record at Princeton was among the best; at graduation, he was among the small group of students who had maintained a grade average of 90 percent or better. As a student, he was already displaying the organized style of work that characterized him throughout his career. He had taken a correspondence course in Graham shorthand—a method, which reduced words and phrases to a series of symbols, enabling a listener to transcribe accurately the words of a rapid speaker. He used the shorthand to make notes on his college lectures. In later life, Wilson often used Graham shorthand to prepare a speech. Then, reading the shorthand, he would tap the speech out on his Hammond portable typewriter. On many occasions, however, he spoke extemporaneously—without a prepared text. Unlike most modern political figures, he never employed a speechwriter.

Although Wilson's academic record at Princeton was good, he probably got more out of his extracurricular activities than from his courses. He read extensively beyond his course requirements. Biographies of political and literary figures attracted him particularly. He organized the Liberal Debating Club and wrote its constitution. In 1877, he won second prize in the sophomore oratorical contest; his subject was "The Ideal Statesman." He worked on the recently established college newspaper, *The Princetonian*, and in his junior year was elected as its managing editor. Athletics interested him, too. However, because of his slender build (he stood just short of six feet and in his senior year weighed 156 pounds) and perhaps for want of outstanding athletic ability, he made no varsity

The Alligator Club was Wilson's eating club while he was an undergraduate at Princeton. He is the member holding his hat in his hand. Years later, Wilson as president of Princeton tried to do away with the eating clubs on the ground that they were snobbish and that membership in them interfered with the academic life of undergraduates. (Library of Congress)

team, but he was elected president of the college baseball organization and secretary of the football association.

Wilson's interest in politics grew rapidly at Princeton. He sometimes told colleagues that he would meet them in the United States Senate, and in one of his books he left a card on which he he had written, "Thomas Woodrow Wilson, Senator from Virginia." He particularly admired the British parliamentary system. In "Cabinet Government in the United States," one of the many essays and magazine articles he wrote as an undergraduate, he called Congress "a deliberative body in which there is little real deliberation"[8] because most of its work was done in committees. Wilson thought that members of the president's cabinet should have seats in Congress, after the British model. Ironically, this article was accepted by a national magazine, the *International Review*, of which Henry Cabot Lodge was a junior editor. As a senator from Massachusetts four decades later, Lodge was the fiercest opponent of Wilson's effort to bring the United States into the League of Nations.

In spite of his successes at Princeton, Wilson felt that he had some limitations. In a letter to his father, he described himself as "a queer fellow," of whom it could be said that

> He is entirely free from anything like his father's clearsightedness and altogether his mind seems to be remarkably bright and empty. You could easily distinguish him in a crowd by his long nose, open mouth, and consequential manner. He is noted in college as a man who can make a remarkably good show with little or no material. But, after all, he is a good enough sort of fellow and what he lacks in solidity he makes up in good intentions and spasmodic endeavors. He has a few queer ideas of his own and very few of them are his own. He writes sometimes but his style lacks clearness and his choice of words is far from good. Ideas are scarce in his compositions and what few there are go limping about in a cloud of wordy expressions and under a heavy weight of lost nouns and adjectives. Ideas are to his writings what oases are to the desert, except that his ideas are very seldom distinguishable from the waste that surrounds them. . . . From what I have seen of him he is apt to allow himself to sympathize almost too heartily with everything that is afloat and, consequently, subjects

his nervous system to frequent severe and, sometimes, rather unnecessary strains.[9]

By the time of graduation, Wilson had decided that the ministry was not the ideal career for a man who was fascinated by government and hoped to become a statesman himself. Law, the career of so many political figures, was a better choice. And so, in the autumn of 1879, he began studies at the University of Virginia's law school. There, as at Princeton, he distinguished himself as a writer and speaker and read extensively beyond his course requirements.

It was characteristic of him to join the university's debating club, the Jefferson Literary Society (of which he eventually became secretary and then president), and to rewrite its constitution. In the society's annual debate of 1880—a big event on campus—he won one of the two prizes offered. First prize was the Debater's Medal and second prize was the Orator's Medal. Wilson had expected to be first but came in second to William Cabell Bruce (later for many years a U.S. senator from Maryland). Wilson's initial reaction was to refuse the prize because, he said, he was a debater, not an orator. In the end, he accepted it, asserting nonetheless that he would do better than Bruce in his career. The episode displayed several traits that would reappear often in Wilson's career: his competitiveness, his tendency to underestimate an opponent and his determination to triumph in the end.

Wilson also showed a side of his personality that contrasted with his usual sober and dignified attitude. Archibald W. Patterson, a fellow student at Virginia and one of Wilson's close friends there, later wrote about Wilson:

> He had an inexhaustible store of anecdotes and was a very prince of story tellers, always suiting the action to the word. When in one of these moods, he was as good as a circus. I often thought what an incomparable actor he would have made. Having a wonderfully mobile countenance, his facial expression at times was too ludicrous for description. On the other hand, when in a more serious vein, he could do the tragic part with equal effect. But he preferred comedy. He loved nothing better than a smart joke. But his jokes were never of the off-color variety. There was such cleaness and propriety in his fun-making

that no one ever ventured to tell a risqué anecdote or use questionable language in his presence. He did not dance, smoke, drink or play cards, yet his attitude toward those who saw fit to indulge in such things had nothing in it of intolerance or censoriousness.[10]

As a law student, however, Wilson found himself "most terribly bored by the noble study of Law." [11] The course work, he said, was about as interesting as eating hash, but he was "swallowing the vast mass of its technicalities with as good a grace and as straight a face as an offended palate will allow." [12]

Before long, however, he had swallowed enough. As at Davidson, he eventually came down with respiratory and digestive trouble. Late in 1880, during his second year at Virginia, he withdrew from the law school and went home, where for the next year and a half he finished his law studies by private reading.

It was during this time that he dropped his first name. He had been moving in that direction, changing his signature from "Thomas W. Wilson" to "T. Woodrow Wilson," and in 1881 he told his Princeton classmate Robert Bridges that he was now Woodrow—no longer Tommy except to his friends. He said he had made the change for his mother's sake, because she was proud of her side of the family—the Woodrow side.

Wilson was apparently a good student of his own teaching, because when he took the bar examination in order to practice law, he achieved one of the highest scores the examining judge had ever seen. When faced with the question of where to practice, Wilson chose Atlanta—partly because it was something of a boom town and partly because he had the opportunity to form a partnership with Edward I. Renick, whom he had known at the University of Virginia. But the firm of Renick & Wilson attracted few clients, and Wilson found both Atlanta and the practice of law unappealing. He was, he said, "buried in humdrum life down here in slow, ignorant, uninteresting Georgia,"[13] and found the concepts of law much more interesting than its "scheming and haggling practice."[14]

One good thing did come of Wilson's law career. Traveling to Rome, Georgia, in the spring of 1883 to do some legal work for his mother, he met and was smitten by Ellen Louise Axson. She was the daughter of the Reverend Samuel Axson, a Pres-

The Glee Club of The Johns Hopkins University posed for this picture when Wilson was a member as a graduate student. He is the second from the left of the six members who are standing; his mustache and long sideburns were a brief affectation and are seen in few other photographs. (Library of Congress)

byterian minister who was an old friend of Wilson's father. Later, Wilson said of Ellen: "I remember thinking 'what a bright, pretty face; what splendid, mischievous, laughing eyes! I'll lay a wager that this demure little lady has lots of life and fun in her!'"[15] He began an ardent courtship, and they were engaged by September.

By that time, Wilson had decided that law practice was not for him, and realized he was meant to be a scholar. What he needed was a career that gave him a steady income with plenty of time and favorable conditions for studying. "What better can I be, therefore," he asked, "than a professor, a lecturer upon subjects whose study delights me?"[16]

And so, in the fall of 1883, Wilson abandoned his law practice and enrolled as a graduate student at Johns Hopkins University in Baltimore to prepare himself for a career in scholarship. His area of study was history and political science.

As usual, Wilson took on more work than his courses required. He set about writing a book on the United States Congress—a work his teachers and fellow students praised so much that he sent a sample to Houghton Mifflin & Company, a publishing company. Houghton Mifflin encouraged Wilson, and in 1885 they published the book as *Congressional Government*. The work was well received and quickly won Wilson a great deal of attention and a reputation as a scholar.

On the same day in January of 1885 that Wilson received the first copies of the finished book from the publisher, he also landed his first job as a college teacher. Starting in September, Wilson would teach history and political science at Bryn Mawr, a newly established women's college near Philadelphia. On the strength of the prospective job and the steady income it would provide— $1,500 a year—he and Ellen Axson were married in June. Wilson's second career and his first family were launched.

Notes

1. David H. Burton, *The Learned Presidency* (Rutherford, N.J.: Fairleigh Dickinson University Press, 1988), p. 138.
2. Arthur S. Link, *Woodrow Wilson: A Brief Biography* (Cleveland: The World Publishing Company, 1963), p. 15.
3. Arthur Walworth, *Woodrow Wilson* (New York: W. W. Norton and Company, 1978), vol. 1, p. 9.
4. Walworth, *Woodrow Wilson*, vol. 1, p. 14.
5. Walworth, *Woodrow Wilson*, vol. 1, p. 16.
6. Bliss Perry, *And Gladly Teach* (Boston: Houghton Mifflin, 1935), p. 153.
7. Edwin A. Weinstein, *Woodrow Wilson: A Medical and Psychological Biography* (Princeton, N.J.: Princeton University Press, 1981), p. 23.
8. Walworth, *Woodrow Wilson*, vol. 1, p. 23.
9. Walworth, *Woodrow Wilson*, vol. 1, p.18.
10. Arthur S. Link, *Woodrow Wilson: A Profile* (New York: Hill and Wang, 1968), pp. 11–12.
11. Arthur S. Link, *Wilson: The Road to the White House*, (Princeton, N.J.: Princeton University Press, 1947), p. 7.
12. Walworth, *Woodrow Wilson*, vol. 1, p. 24.
13. Walworth, *Woodrow Wilson*, vol. 1, p. 34.

14. Walworth, *Woodrow Wilson*, vol. 1, p. 34.
15. Weinstein, *Woodrow Wilson: A Medical and Psychological Biography*, p. 56.
16. Walworth, *Woodrow Wilson*, vol. 1, p. 35.

THE EDUCATOR
(1885–1910)

B ryn Mawr College was a most modest institution in 1885, with 42 students and two buildings. Wilson, as a one-man department of history and political science, had to work hard. His course topics ranged through ancient and medieval history, modern European and American history and the history of constitutional law. At first, Wilson relished the work. "I am enjoying it, improving under it, and find the girls interested and intelligent," he wrote to a friend.[1] The students, for their part, found his lectures absorbing and admired his witty style.

In 1886, Wilson persuaded Johns Hopkins University to grant him a scholar's most advanced degree, doctor of philosophy (Ph.D.), without further course work or the usually required doctoral thesis. The university accepted his achievement with *Congressional Government* in place of a thesis. In 1887, Wilson signed a contract to remain at Bryn Mawr for another two years. But by that time, he was becoming dissatisfied with his life. His family had grown to include two daughters—Margaret, born in 1886, and Jessie, born in 1887—and the salary of $1,500 a year was insufficient. Moreover, his view of teaching women had changed. Wilson felt that the women in his classes responded weakly to his efforts to draw them into intelligent discussions. Whereas in his first year he found the students interested and intelligent, Wilson wrote now that "lecturing to young women of the present generation on the history and principles of politics" was like "lecturing to stone-masons on the history of fashion and dress."[2] He was, he said, "hungry for a class of *men*."[3]

Wilson got his wish in 1888, when Wesleyan University, a men's college in Connecticut, offered him the Hedding Professorship of History and Political Economy at a considerable increase in salary. Bryn Mawr tried to hold Wilson to his contract but finally allowed him to resign.

Teaching courses in political science and the history of England, France and the United States, Wilson was immensely popular at Wesleyan, as he was everywhere he taught. In addition to his teaching, he helped to coach the football team. Wilson also finished writing a textbook, published by D. C. Heath, called *The State*, which one writer has called "probably Wilson's greatest scholarly achievement."[4] And it was during his stay at Wesleyan that Eleanor Wilson, the family's third and last child, was born in 1889.

But Wesleyan could not keep Wilson when, in 1890, the College of New Jersey offered him a professorship of jurisprudence and political economy. The chance to return to Princeton was irresistible. "I find," he wrote to his father shortly after the offer came, "that everybody regards my election to Princeton as a sort of crowning success."[5]

A success he was—certainly with Princeton students, who repeatedly voted him the college's most popular professor. His lectures, well organized and well presented, drew crowds of students. Wilson also was a master of the enriching anecdote. "Long after other memories of college courses had faded," a biographer wrote, "Princeton alumni remembered his thrilling descriptions of such events as the signing of the Covenant."[6] One of his students said: "His lectures were fascinating, and held me spellbound; each was an almost perfect essay in itself, well rounded and with a distinct literary style."[7] William Starr Myers, who came to Princeton as a teaching assistant to Wilson and later was himself a professor there for many years, declared that "after experience with some very great teachers, I consider Wilson the greatest classroom lecturer I have ever heard."[8] Unlike many other professors, Wilson always kept an open-door policy at home for students who wanted to talk with him.

Soon Wilson was the most highly paid professor at Princeton. Because of his growing reputation, he received alluring offers from a number of other universities—including invitations to become president of the universities of Illinois, Alabama, Minnesota, Virginia, Nebraska and Washington. In order to fend off such offers, a group of wealthy alumni agreed in 1898 to supplement Wilson's yearly salary of $3,000 by $2,400 annually in exchange for his agreement to stay at Princeton for the next five years.

Wilson also supplemented his income by writing. Among other works, he wrote a biography of George Washington and a five-volume *A History of the American People.* Years later, he said of the *History*: "I will tell you frankly, if you will not let it go further, that I wrote it, not to instruct anybody else, but to instruct myself. . . . That may be an expensive process for other persons who bought the book, but I lived in the United States and my interest in learning their history was, not to remember what happened, but to find which way we were going."[9]

The *History* is characteristic of Wilson's precise but perhaps dramatic style of writing. Here is how he described the assassination of President Lincoln five days after the end of the Civil War:

> And then, at the end, when the terrible days were over and a healing time of peace at hand in which passion might run cool again and men remember their common ties of citizenship and fraternity, a deeply tragical thing happened, as if to fill the cup of sectional bitterness to the brim and mark forever the fatal distemper of civil strife. On the evening of the 14th of April, 1865, five days after General Lee's surrender at Appomattox, ere [Confederate General] Johnston had yielded to [Union General] Sherman, Mr. Lincoln was shot in his box at Ford's Theatre in Washington, and the next day lay dead. The assassin had been John Wilkes Booth, the distinguished actor, half crazed by blind enthusiasm and poignant regret for the lost southern cause.[10]

It was a dignified style. Wilson was always dignified in public, sedate even as he pedaled his bicycle around the Princeton campus. He took his bicycle to the White House in 1913 but found that he was too busy and too conspicuous to use it. It would be years before he owned an automobile, and that was one he bought after he left the White House. Indeed, during his Princeton years he had a low opinion of the motor car. Cars were noisy and smelly, he thought, and made bicycling difficult. "I think that of all the menaces of to-day," he said in 1906, "the worst is the reckless driving in automobiles."[11] In later life, however, he came to enjoy automobile rides and took one almost every day.

Dignified though he was in public, he had a lighter side, seen regularly by his family. His daughter Eleanor has left a picture of Wilson as a father:

> He played fascinating games with us in those early days. Suddenly and magically he would blow out his cheeks until his face became a great round balloon which I was permitted to put gently back into shape. He could do the most amazing things with his face. He could gather one cheek in his fingers and pull it out and out like stretched rubber until we screamed in nervous delight. He could drop his chin lower and lower and incredibly lower until we covered our eyes in terror—certain that at last it would touch the floor.
>
> Slapping his hands on his knees, he did the galloping horse. Nearer and nearer, louder and louder, faster and faster, came the sound of the hoof beats until the horse was upon us—then it turned and galloped away—the sound gradually fading in the distance. . . .
>
> [To me] the most enchanting memory of our childhood—[is] father, sitting by the nursery fire singing "Sweet and Low," "Watchman, Tell us of the night." . . . His voice grew softer and softer—farther and farther away—and we slept.[12]

But Wilson's lighter side was seen mostly at home. To the public, Wilson was a serious man whose career was advancing rapidly, as reflected in the *New York Times* on June 10, 1903. An item on the first page began as follows:

> The most noteworthy event of the commencement exercises at Princeton University this year, and the greatest surprise of many years, was announced this afternoon [June 9] at the annual meeting of the Board of Trustees,

when President Francis Lander Patton resigned and Woodrow Wilson, Professor of Politics and Jurisprudence, was elected to fill the vacancy.[13]

"This thing," Wilson said in a speech at the graduation ceremonies on June 10, "came like a thunderbolt out of a clear sky."[14] Wilson may have been surprised, but he was prepared for the task and bursting with ideas. His primary goal was to make Princeton a first-class academic institution—a place where the emphasis was not on how to earn a living but on showing young men the richness of knowledge. "We must not lose sight," he said at his inauguration as Princeton's president, "of that fine conception of a general training which led our fathers."[15]

To that end, Wilson quickly told the trustees what he thought the university needed and what the program would cost. His list began with what he called the preceptorial system, a new method of teaching undergraduates; he would need $2,250,000 to launch it. The other items included $1,000,000 for a school of science, $2,750,000 for new buildings and increases in the teaching staff, $3,000,000 for a graduate school, $2,400,000 for a school of jurisprudence, $750,000 for a school of electrical engineering and $500,000 for a museum of natural history.

The preceptors Wilson had in mind would be young scholars who would live closely with the undergraduates and help them with their studies. "If we could get a body of such tutors at Princeton," he said, "we could transform the place from a place where there are youngsters doing tasks to a place where there are men doing thinking."[16]

Wilson helped to raise the money for the program and interviewed the applicants himself. Soon he had attracted fifty bright young men to the university. Many of them went on to become outstanding scholars and teachers. "Never," a Princeton professor has said, "has so much life and vigor been injected at one stroke into an established university faculty."[17] This system remains in operation at Princeton today.

Wilson's next move was to reorganize the course of study. Freshmen and sophomores would take required courses. Then they would choose a major subject on which they would

"Prospect," the name of this mansion, was the official residence of Princeton University's president when this photograph was taken in 1903. Wilson, his wife and their three daughters moved into it in 1902, after his election as president of the university. The house still stands but is now used as a conference center. (Library of Congress)

concentrate for the next two years, taking at the same time elective courses in other subjects. This program was so successful that Harvard and Yale soon adopted similar programs, and it is the basis of most undergraduate programs today.

It was a time of triumph and happiness for Wilson. The presidency of Princeton carried with it the occupancy of the biggest house the Wilsons had ever lived in—an architectural pile named Prospect. But the Wilsons made a home of it, and Wilson particularly enjoyed his workroom in the mansion's square tower. Eleanor Wilson described a typical family scene at Prospect:

> Nearly every evening, and often at meals, there were heated arguments or long discussions about the meaning of some word or the exact significance of some phrase and, before these questions were settled to the satisfaction of everyone, there were sometimes eight or nine books of reference on the floor beside his chair.[18]

She also described the family's singular way of celebrating the arrival of a new year at Prospect:

> We always had a rollicking New Year's Eve. Following an old Scottish custom, we gathered in the dining room and, standing on our chairs with one foot on the table, sang "Auld Lang Syne" at the top of our voices and drank a toast. Then we dashed to open the front door and let the Old Year out and the New Year in.[19]

The preceptorial system and the new course of study were highly regarded at Princeton and made Wilson a great success. They also gained him a national reputation. "Had he resigned the presidency of the University in 1905," one of his biographers has written, "his educational reputation would have been secured and it could then have been said that no man, in Princeton's one hundred and sixty years of existence, had made a greater contribution to the University's progress and greatness."[20] But Wilson went on to attempt some further innovations that landed him in trouble.

One of them was an attack on Princeton's eating clubs. They were similar to fraternity houses in that students lived and ate there. But there was stiff competition to get into an eating club, and many students failed. "The tragedy of the unchosen was repeated every year," Eleanor Wilson wrote, "and many a student's life in college, and even afterward, was injured by what almost amounted to social ostracism."[21]

Wilson thought the clubs emphasized the social side of university life and interfered with the academic side. He proposed to replace them with what he called quadrangles. A quadrangle would be a self-contained living unit with its own dining hall, library and common rooms. Students of all the classes would live there along with young and unmarried members of the faculty. The plan was modeled on the colleges of Oxford and Cambridge Universities in England.

Wilson had not reckoned with the devotion of Princeton alumni to their eating clubs. Their objections defeated the plan. Harvard and Yale adopted similar plans in the 1930s—Harvard calls its institutions houses and Yale calls them colleges—but to this day Princeton has its eating clubs.

Another controversy arose over where to build a new graduate school. Wilson wanted it to be on the campus. The graduate dean, Andrew F. West, wanted it to be separate. The battle over this issue went on for years and turned into a personal feud between Wilson and West. In the end, Wilson lost, mainly because prominent alumni willing to provide money for the school sided with West.

By 1910, Wilson had become a controversial figure at Princeton. He no longer had the wholehearted support of the trustees and faculty, and his tenure seemed to be in jeopardy. But Wilson's troubles at Princeton had not affected his growing national reputation as a leader of distinction, and some prominent Democrats in New Jersey had begun talking of him as a possible nominee for governor. His third career was about to begin.

Notes

1. Edwin A. Weinstein, *Woodrow Wilson: A Medical and Psychological Biography* (Princeton, N.J.: Princeton University Press, 1981), p. 90.
2. Weinstein, *Woodrow Wilson: A Medical and Psychological Biography*, p. 93.
3. Arthur Walworth, *Woodrow Wilson* (New York: W. W. Norton and Company, 1978), vol. 1, p. 50.
4. Arthur S. Link, *Wilson: The Road to the White House* (Princeton, N.J.: Princeton University Press, 1947), p. 21.
5. Walworth, *Woodrow Wilson*, vol. 1, p. 53.
6. Weinstein, *Woodrow Wilson: A Medical and Psychological Biography*, p. 109.
7. John A. Garraty, *Woodrow Wilson* (Westport, Conn.: Greenwood Press, 1977), p. 17.
8. Arthur S. Link, ed., *Woodrow Wilson: A Profile* (New York: Hill and Wang, 1968), p. 39.
9. Garraty, *Woodrow Wilson*, pp. 24–25.
10. Woodrow Wilson, *A History of the American People* (New York: Harper and Brothers, 1902), vol. IV, p. 259.
11. Weinstein, *Woodrow Wilson: A Medical and Psychological Biography*, p. 135.
12. Eleanor Wilson McAdoo, *The Woodrow Wilsons* (New York: Macmillan, 1937),pp. 3–5.

13. *The New York Times*, June 10, 1902, p. 1.
14. *The New York Times*, June 11, 1902, p. 2.
15. Link, *Wilson: The Road to the White House*, p. 38.
16. Link, *Wilson: The Road to the White House*, p. 40.
17. Link, *Wilson: The Road to the White House*, p. 43.
18. McAdoo, *The Woodrow Wilsons*, p. 69.
19. McAdoo, *The Woodrow Wilsons*, p. 75.
20. Link, *Wilson: The Road to the White House*, p. 43.
21. McAdoo, *The Woodrow Wilsons*, p. 97.

THE GOVERNOR
(1910–1913)

New Jersey in 1910 was run by political bosses and the
big corporations whose interests the bosses protected.
Political bosses in those days were men who had worked
hard for their party and had come to be recognized as party
leaders. They seldom held elective offices themselves but
worked behind the scenes. The Democratic leaders, powerful
in their own counties, had been out of power at the state level
for years and were eager to find a candidate for governor who
might return the party to power in the statehouse at Trenton.
They wanted a man who would be appealing to the voters but
could be trusted to take orders from the bosses if he became
governor. Wilson, prominent in the academic world but without political experience, looked like such a man.

The principal figure in this quest was James Smith, Jr., boss
of the Newark-Essex County political machine. Smith was a
wealthy banker and publisher who looked like a political boss:
portly, well dressed and with an air of command. He had been
a U.S. senator from New Jersey between 1893 and 1899 and
entertained notions of being returned to that post if the Democrats gained control of the state. (In those days, members of
the U.S. Senate were chosen by the state legislatures; they
were not elected by popular vote until after the adoption of the
17th amendment to the U. S. Constitution in 1913.)

Smith decided that Wilson was the man who should be the party's nominee for governor. He had the political clout to enforce his choice, and Wilson was duly nominated in September. Soon thereafter, Wilson resigned from his post at Princeton in order to concentrate on getting elected to the governorship. Out on the campaign trail, Wilson told the voters: "If you give me your votes I will be under bond to you—not to the gentlemen who were generous enough to nominate me."[1] Those gentlemen did not take him seriously; a candidate was expected to say such things.

Nor were the Democrats greatly concerned when Wilson campaigned for major reforms: direct public election of senators, creation of a public service commission to regulate the rates of the powerful companies that provided such services as electricity and public transportation, primary elections to choose candidates for public office instead of having candidates picked by the bosses. It was all window dressing, the party leaders thought; once Wilson was in office, he could be persuaded to drop the idea of reform.

What the leaders failed to appreciate was that a large number of voters—Democrats, Republicans and independents —were tired of boss rule, rigged elections and heavy-handed corporations. Those voters formed what would come to be called the "Progressive movement." Wilson aimed his appeal at this bloc of voters, and they carried him into office. He won the governorship handily in November of 1910, and on the strength of his popularity the Democrats won control of both houses of the state legislature.

Wilson had to show even before his inauguration that he would not be the puppet of the bosses. Once it was clear that the Democrats would control the legislature, Smith made known his expectation to be returned to the U. S. Senate. But there was a complication. In 1907, New Jersey had adopted a law allowing candidates for the Senate to put their names before the public in what was called a preferential primary election. Winning such an election would not necessarily mean anything, since senators were still chosen by the state legislature. But in 1910, the self-styled "Farmer Orator" James E. Martine entered the Democratic primary and won. Martine was an undistinguished political figure; he had run twice for a seat in the U. S. House of Representatives, three times for the state senate, four times for the state assembly and twice for governor, losing every time. He was now the man the Democratic voters had backed for the Senate.

What was Wilson to do? He had campaigned for primary elections as a means of choosing candidates, and Martine had won what might be called a demonstration primary. Wilson could not laugh him off. Nor could he afford being seen by the Progressives as giving in to Smith. Wilson began working hard among the newly elected members of the legislature to have Martine chosen for the Senate, and he prevailed.

This victory established Wilson as the leader of the New Jersey Democrats. It also gained him national attention. Newspapers throughout the country had followed the senatorial fight, and many of them had published editorials supporting Wilson's position.

At that time, New Jersey did not provide the governor with a governor's mansion, and so the Wilson family had to move first into a small suite of rooms at the Princeton Inn and then into a house on Cleveland Lane in Princeton—a comfortable house, but far smaller than Prospect. The state did provide the governor with an oceanside summer home at Sea Girt, but there Wilson was expected to review periodically the troops marching on a nearby parade ground. Moreover, he was expected to do so while mounted on a horse and wearing an unlikely riding costume: a frock coat and a top hat. It was a memorable scene.

As governor, Wilson quickly established an orderly routine. He occupied a large but rather gloomy office in the state capitol—a room lined with law books and portraits of former governors and also displaying a bronze bust of George Washington. There Wilson turned first each morning to his correspondence. In those days, when the telephone was still a new device, public figures conducted much of their business by mail. Wilson tried another new instrument, the Dictaphone, but did not like the way his voice sounded on it and reverted to typing drafts of his letters or dictating to a secretary. On some days he dictated a hundred letters or more in one morning. Many letters went to people with whom his politically wise private secretary, Joseph P. Tumulty, advised him to cultivate a relationship. In the afternoon, Wilson held conferences, talked

Wilson as governor of New Jersey in 1911 and 1912 had as his secretary and political adviser Joseph P. Tumulty, a former member of the New Jersey State Assembly who went on to the White House with Wilson and remained close to him for many years. Here Tumulty watches as the governor prepares to sign a document. (Library of Congress)

with visitors and sometimes strolled into the outer office to chat with people who had turned up there.

As soon as Wilson took office in January 1911, he began pushing the program of reforms he had presented during the campaign. Reasoning with the legislators, cajoling them, threatening when he had to, leading them as though he were a prime minister in a parliament, he pushed through four major bills in a space of three months. The first one established primary elections as the means of choosing candidates in New Jersey. Then came a corrupt practices act that struck against voting frauds and the bribery of public officials. Another bill established a Public Utility Commission with power to control the rates and services of gas and electric companies, railroads, streetcar and bus systems, water companies, telephone and telegraph systems and other utilities. A workmen's compensation bill provided for a system of accident insurance for workers injured on the job. On its own initiative, the legislature adopted several other reforms. It was an impressive achievement. George L. Record, a New Jersey Republican interested in reform, called it "the most remarkable record of progressive legislation ever known in the political history of this or any other State."[2] The *Jersey Journal* said:

> On the Governor's side, the fight for progressive legislation in redemption of platform promises was perhaps the most scientific political battle ever waged in New Jersey. . . . The victory Governor Wilson has won is a revelation of the man's character and leadership and a marvel to the country. No Governor has ever achieved so much in so short a time. In less than four months he has turned New Jersey from one of the most conservative and machine-dominated states into a leader in the forefront of progressive commonwealths.[3]

The achievement was also widely noticed elsewhere in the country. Many people began to talk of Wilson as the man the Democrats should nominate for president in 1912. The thought was put in writing by William C. Liller, president of the National Democratic League of Clubs:

> I believe that the party in order to win next year must be PROGRESSIVE and not reactionary and that it must

Wilson as governor made good use of the telephone, then a fairly recent innovation, to keep in touch with political associates and members of the legislature as he pushed a bold reform program through the state's law-making process. He always wore glasses after his youth, and except on rare occasions, they were of this "pince-nez" (French for "pinch-nose") type. (Library of Congress)

> select as its standard bearers men who can command the united Democratic support and that of thousands of voters of independence and courage. That is to say I want to see the [nominating] convention name you for President.[4]

Wilson was definitely interested. He adopted the presidential hopeful's practice of going on speaking trips to other parts of the country as a means of making himself more widely known and establishing contacts with influential Democrats. Several of his supporters started putting together an organization to run and raise money for his campaign. Wilson-for-President clubs sprang up all over the country. By the end of 1911, the campaign was at full boil.

And a campaign was essential, for Wilson had serious competition. The main competitor was James Beauchamp "Champ" Clark, Speaker of the U.S. House of Representatives. Clark was a seasoned politician from Missouri with a long record of progressivism. A journalist described him in 1912:

A human, likeable old gentleman . . . pleasant to talk with or to listen to, popular, magnetic, devoted to his books and his home and his family. . . . An interesting personality, that of Champ Clark—and if he has any conception of the vital, burning questions the American people are asking, any grasp on the issues and problems on which the voters of the nation are sharply divided. . . . any comprehension of the great readjustments that are going on across party lines as the Progressives and Conservatives are reclassifying themselves, one finds no evidence of it in his conversation or recorded speeches.[5]

Clark was, as another writer put it, "something of a party hack" and "neither an aggressive leader nor an original thinker."[6] Nevertheless, he had a substantial following among Democrats and also the support of the powerful newspaper and magazine publisher William R. Hearst.

Two other candidates also had significant support. Oscar W. Underwood of Alabama, chairman of the tax-writing Ways and Means Committee of the U. S. House of Representatives, was the first Southerner since the Civil War to try for the Democratic presidential nomination. And Judson Harmon, governor of Ohio, had gained attention as one of the new leaders of the Democratic party.

Throughout the first half of 1912, the candidates and their supporters maneuvered to line up delegates committed to vote for them, at least in the early stages, at the Democratic national convention in Baltimore that summer. The convention was, as always, a scene of long and windy speeches followed by long and noisy demonstrations in favor of one candidate or another. On the first ballot, Clark had 440½ votes; Wilson, 324; Harmon, 148; and Underwood, 117½. Clark's total was impressive but well short of the two-thirds vote required for the nomination. The voting went on for days, with much wheeling and dealing behind the scenes. At times Clark had a majority of the votes but still not enough for nomination. At one point, Wilson, thinking the trend was toward Clark, sent a telegram saying he would withdraw his name from the balloting. His supporter William G. McAdoo, a prominent lawyer and businessman from New York, persuaded him to stay in the race. Finally, on the 46th ballot, enough supporters dropped away from Clark to give Wilson the nomination.

His campaign almost immediately got an enormous boost when the Republican Party split between supporters of Theodore Roosevelt and William Howard Taft. Roosevelt, president of the United States from 1901 to 1909, spoke for a large group of Progressives. Taft, his successor as president from 1909 to 1913, had displeased Roosevelt by ineffective leadership. In August 1912, a convention of Progressives voted to form a third party with Roosevelt as its nominee for president. Roosevelt, accepting the nomination, said he felt like a "bull moose," and the name stuck to his third-party movement.

The Republicans nominated Taft. It was quickly clear that the race would be between Wilson and Roosevelt. Taft, writing to his wife, said as early as July that he might as well give up because "there are so many people in the country who don't like me."[7] Wilson too saw that the contest was between him and Roosevelt. Writing to his friend Mary Allen Hulbert Peck in August, he said just that and added:

> I am by no means confident. He appeals to their [the public's] imagination; I do not. He is a real, vivid person, whom they have seen and shouted themselves hoarse over and voted for, millions strong; I am a vague, conjectural personality, more made up of opinions and academic prepossessions than of human traits and red corpuscles.[8]

Wilson and Roosevelt campaigned for similar goals beloved by Progressives, chief among them being a means of controlling monopoly practices by corporations. Wilson called his program the "New Freedom"; Roosevelt named his the "New Nationalism." The publisher William Allen White later wrote: "Between the New Nationalism and the New Freedom was that fantastic imaginary gulf that always has existed between tweedle-dum and tweedle-dee."[9]

In the end, the election turned on how people viewed the two personalities. Roosevelt as president had been a blustering, militaristic figure and was seen by many as an impulsive man, who might lead the nation into some regretted adventure. Wilson impressed people as rational and deliberate. The vote in November was 6,293,019 for Wilson and 4,119,507 for Roosevelt. The Democrats also took control of both houses of

Congress, smoothing the path for Wilson to press his reform program when he took office.

A month after the election, Wilson was honored in Staunton, Virginia, the city of his birth. While he was there, he called on an elderly aunt who still lived there. Eleanor Wilson tells of the meeting:

> She was very old and deaf, and used a long black ear-trumpet. After a few minutes of rather difficult conversation, she asked kindly, "Well, Tommy, what are you doing now?" Father said modestly, "I've been elected President, Aunt Janie." "What?" "President." "Well, well," said the old lady querulously, "president of what?" Father seized the trumpet desperately and roared into its black depths, "President of the United States," whereupon she smiled skeptically and dismissed him."[10]

Wilson had four months (slightly more than the two later provided for in the 20th amendment to the Constitution, adopted in 1933) between the election and his inauguration. He used the time to choose his cabinet and plan the opening moves of his administration. In both of these tasks he had the crucial advice of Edward M. House, a man he had met during the campaign. House was a wealthy, retiring Texan—endowed by Texas with the honorary title of colonel, which he disliked—with good political connections and a keen sense of what was smart politics. Wilson and House became good friends. "You are the only person in the world with whom I can discuss everything," Wilson once said. "There are some I can tell one thing and others another, but you are the only one to whom I can make an entire clearance of mind."[11] House was to be Wilson's closest adviser during almost all of the administration that was about to begin.

Notes

1. Gene Smith, *When the Cheering Stopped* (New York: William Morrow and Company, 1964), p. 29.
2. Arthur S. Link, *Woodrow Wilson: A Brief Biography* (Cleveland: The World Publishing Company, 1963), p. 48.

3. Arthur S. Link, *Wilson: The Road to the White House* (Princeton, N.J.: Princeton University Press, 1947), p. 273.

4. Link, *Wilson: The Road to the White House*, p. 312.

5. Frank Parker Stockbridge, "Champ Clark of Pike County," *The World's Work*, May 1912, p. 36.

6. Link, *Wilson: The Road to the White House*, p. 401.

7. Link, *Wilson: The Road to the White House*, p. 475.

8. Link, *Wilson: The Road to the White House,* p. 475.

9. William Allen White, *Woodrow Wilson* (Boston: Houghton Mifflin, 1924), p. 264.

10. Eleanor Wilson McAdoo, *The Woodrow Wilsons* (New York: Macmillan, 1937), p. 195.

11. Arthur S. Link, *Wilson: The New Freedom* (Princeton, N.J.: Princeton University Press, 1956), p. 93.

4

THE PREWAR PRESIDENT (1913–1917)

Inauguration Day, March 4, 1913, was a Tuesday that dawned cloudy. But at midday, during the climax of the inaguration ceremonies, the sun broke through—a good omen, some said, for the administration of the first Democrat to be sworn in as president since Grover Cleveland began his second term in 1897. Cleveland, who had been a Princeton trustee during Wilson's time as president of the university, was the only two-term president whose terms were not consecutive. In 1892, the last year of his first term, he ran for reelection but lost to Benjamin Harrison even though his popular vote was larger than Harrison's. In 1896, he ran again and defeated Harrison. The interruption in terms created a problem for president counters. In his first term, Cleveland was the 22nd man to become president. Harrison was the 23rd. So how should one count Cleveland when he began his second term? The State Department had to make a ruling; it decided that Cleveland in his second term was the nation's 24th president.

In keeping with tradition, Wilson had called at the White House shortly before noon on Inauguration Day. There President Taft greeted him, and the two men—top-hatted and frock-coated—rode to the Capitol building together in an open carriage drawn by four horses. Because of the crowds and the ceremonial pace, the trip took 40 minutes, almost twice as long as it would take an able person to cover the mile and a half at a brisk walk.

Wilson took the oath of office from Chief Justice Edward D. White and then stepped to the lectern at the east front of the Capitol to make his inaugural address. There he saw that the soldiers in attendance had kept spectators out of a large area in front of the inaugural stand. Disapproving, he issued his first order as president: "Let the people come forward!"[1] They did, and he then made a short but eloquent inaugural address. The nation had become great, but, he said:

> There has been something crude and heartless and unfeeling in our haste to succeed and be great. Our thought has been "Let every man look out for himself, let every generation look out for itself," while we reared giant machinery which made it impossible that any but those who stood at the levers of control should have a chance to look out for themselves. . . .
>
> We have come now to the sober second thought. The scales of heedlessness have fallen from our eyes. We have made up our minds to square every process of our National life again with the standards we so proudly set up at the beginning and have always carried at our hearts. Our work is a work of restoration.[2]

And he ticked off several "things that ought to be altered."[3] Among them were the tariff, the banking and currency system and monopolistic business practices.

For the Wilsons, moving into the White House meant a new style of living. The family that had not owned an automobile now had a fleet of them available, all with drivers. The family that had managed much of the time with no servants now had a large household staff, headed by Irwin H. "Ike" Hoover, who held the title of chief usher. Hoover, who started at the White House as an electrician in 1891, continued there until his death in 1933, serving under nine presidents. In a memoir published after his death, he called Wilson the "most intelligent" and "most satisfactory to work with"[4] of the nine presidents.

Characteristically, Wilson promptly established a work routine that he seldom varied. He would have his standard breakfast of two raw eggs in grape juice, followed by hot cereal and coffee. Appearing in his office promptly at 9:00 A.M., he read his mail and dictated letters for an hour. For the next three hours, until lunch, he talked with visitors or held cabinet meetings. After lunch he had two more hours of appointments and then went to play golf or take an automobile ride. (He was an enthusiastic but poor golfer averaging about 115 strokes for 18 holes.) Evenings he reserved for his family.

At first, Wilson used the meetings with his cabinet members to get input from them on different issues of importance. Josephus Daniels, secretary of the navy, described a typical session:

> As President Wilson took his seat at the head of the table, he looked the moderator, fitting into place and power. His plan from the first was to present some matter or matters about which he desired what he was fond of calling

The cabinet assembled by Wilson after his election as president of the United States in 1912 posed for this photograph at one of its early meetings. The man to Wilson's immediate right is William Jennings Bryan, secretary of state, who had run unsuccessfully as the Democratic nominee for president in 1896, 1900 and 1908. To Wilson's immediate left is William Gibbs McAdoo, secretary of the treasury, who later married Wilson's youngest daughter, Eleanor.
(Library of Congress)

"common counsel," and after he had received the reaction of Cabinet members, his practice was to call on each member to present any question that concerned departmental policies, for debate and exchange of news. . . . He never took a vote, pursuing a course, as he often said, more like a Quaker meeting, in which after full discussion the President would say, "It seems to me the sense of the meeting is so and so," and the policy thus ascertained would be the program of the administration.[5]

But the president soon found that reports of the discussions were leaking to newspaper reporters. The leaker turned out to be Franklin K. Lane, secretary of the interior. As a result, Wilson stopped discussing important matters at cabinet meetings, and the meetings became what Lindley M. Garrison, the secretary of war, called an interesting waste of time.

Wilson's reaction to the leaks reflected his difficult relations with the press. He had hoped otherwise. Announcing early in his term a plan to hold regular news conferences, he did so for a while but found them disagreeable and eventually abandoned them. Arthur Krock, Washington correspondent of the *New York Times* for many years, declared that Wilson "is the most inaccessible executive of recent times and the weekly conferences with him develop no news whatever as he simply parries all questions."[6]

In individual interviews, however, Wilson could be charming and informative. The reporter William Bayard Hale of *World's Work*, calling the president "the best listener that has been in the White House for many a year,"[7] described how a typical visitor fared:

An interview with Mr. Wilson is always a delightful and satisfactory affair. Not always, of course, in its results, for the United States now has a President who can say "no" as easily as "yes," though he knows how to take the sting out of a refusal, if he wants to. But an interview is always delightful and satisfactory in that the visitor has the fullest opportunity to tell his story and make his request or his argument, assured of an attentive hearing. All visitors agree that Mr. Wilson has a peculiar faculty of putting them at their best; not a few timid, unready talkers have told me wonderingly that in his company they found their tongues unloosed and their ideas flowing rapidly into

Ellen Axson Wilson, Wilson's first wife and the mother of Margaret, Jessie and Eleanor, stands at her husband's side in this rather formal portrait photograph. She died in the White House of kidney disease only 17 months after Wilson became president, leaving him so grief stricken that he had trouble carrying on with his duties. (Library of Congress)

> appropriate words. . . . He is a shy man himself, if the truth
> were known, and perhaps it is the most timid of men who
> are the best understood by him.[8]

When he began his presidency, Wilson was still suffering
from the headaches and digestive upsets that had plagued him
for years. Indeed, he had such a spell at the end of inauguration
week, apparently because he had been through such an ordeal
of speechmaking and handshaking. Fortunately, a physician
who would make a great difference in Wilson's life was at hand.
Cary T. Grayson, a medical officer in the navy, had served Taft
as White House physician, and on Taft's recommendation
Wilson kept the young doctor on in the same job. Grayson
attended Wilson five days after the inauguration and later
wrote:

> This was the beginning of my diagnosis of his general
> condition and my systematic treatment which depended
> very little on drugs. Indeed, when I took his medicines
> away from him he accused me of being a "therapeutic
> nihilist." It seemed to me a clear case for preventive
> medicine. I was able to get his cooperation in my plans
> through a simple appeal to his reason. I reminded him that
> he had four hard years ahead of him and that he owed it
> to himself and the American people to get into as fit
> condition as possible and to stay there. The regime in-
> cluded plenty of fresh air, a diet suited to his idiosyncracies
> as I discovered them, plenty of sleep, daily motor rides,
> occasional trips on the *Mayflower* [the presidential yacht],
> and especially regular games of golf, together with treat-
> ment for a persistent case of neuritis from which he had
> long suffered.
> By reason of his outdoor recreation and exercise, I was
> quickly drawn into close, personal association with him,
> for I was his regular companion in these diversions.[9]

Grayson and Wilson became close friends and frequent com-
panions despite the difference of 22 years in their ages. In his
memoir, Grayson described the closeness of the relationship,
writing of how Wilson "opened his mind to me as to no one else,
except his wife, not only on public matters, but on literature,
which he loved dearly, and in reminiscence of past experiences,
as Governor of New Jersey, as President of Princeton Univer-

sity, as a professor in Princeton, Wesleyan and Bryn Mawr." Grayson also described Wilson's attitude toward his father, "who had been his chief teacher, and the man of all the world whom he most admired and loved." And Grayson remembered that Wilson had a lighter side: "Gayety of spirits, puns, anecdotes, limericks garnished his graver conversation, so that I became familiar with his lighter moods as well as his more weighty thoughts."[10]

Grayson was probably the only person outside Wilson's family to realize how attached the president was to routines—rereading favorite books, following a fixed set of routes on automobile rides, wearing a particular gray sweater that he had bought while bicycling in Scotland as a young man. "He had no craving for novelty but liked to do the same things over and over again," Grayson said.[11]

Even before he began to benefit from Grayson's regime of diet and exercise, Wilson launched his New Freedom program of reforms. His first target was the tariff.

The tariff was actually a set of tariffs—charges laid on goods imported from other countries. If a foreign manufacturer's list price for an item was $100, the tariff might make its selling price in the United States $140 or more, depending on the size of the tariff levy. Tariffs had provoked endless political battles extending over many decades. Many American manufacturers and regions wanted the tariff to be high to protect their own products against those imported from abroad. The Republican Party in general had favored high tariffs. Importers and people hurt or annoyed by the artifically high price of foreign goods resulting from the tariff, argued for low tariffs as a means of stimulating economic competition. The Democratic Party in general had favored low tariffs, and Wilson was squarely in that camp.

To begin his attack, Wilson decided on the dramatic step of speaking to Congress in person. No president had done that since John Adams, who served from 1797 to 1801. All of Adams's successors, until Wilson, had dealt with Congress by sending written messages. Wilson, appearing before the Senate and the House assembled together in the House chamber on April 8, 1913, said he had come in person because he wanted to show that he was a human being and not "a mere department of the Government hailing Congress from some isolated island of jealous power, sending messages, not speaking naturally with his own voice."[12] (After this appearance, Wilson spoke personally to Congress many more times, making this a common practice by his successors.)

It did Wilson no harm that first time that he made his points clearly and eloquently, taking only 10 minutes to do so. His key point was: "We must abolish everything that bears even the semblance of privilege or of any kind of artificial advantage, and put our businessmen and producers under the stimulation of a constant necessity to be efficient, economical, and enterprising, masters of competitive supremacy, better workers and merchants than any in the world."[13]

The battle in Congress was long and complicated. Senators from states producing wool and sugar were under particularly heavy pressure to resist lowered tariffs. Wilson worked closely with members of Congress to put his program through and eventually succeeded. The new law reduced tariffs on some 900 items and lowered the average tariff rate from 40 percent to about 25 percent. It also established an income tax (made possible by the recently adopted 16th amendment to the Constitution) to make up for the revenue the government would lose because of the reduced tariffs. Wilson signed the bill on October 3, 1913, saying: "I have had the accomplishment of something like this at heart since I was a boy."[14] One of his biographers wrote of Wilson's achievement on the tariff: "A signal triumph, it increased Wilson's standing with the people, and what was of more practical importance at the moment, gave him firm control over his party in Congress."[15]

Wilson needed that control to put through his second major reform, directed at the nation's banking and currency system—essentially the money supply. The banking system, basically unchanged since the Civil War, was really not a system but a collection of some 7,000 banks operating more or less independently. As a result, there was no consistent plan for controlling money reserves, interest rates or the making of loans. The greatest influence on the system came from what was known as the Money Trust—the big banking houses centered on Wall Street in New York, notably J. P. Morgan & Company. Wilson declared his objective to be providing for "public instead of private control, thus making the banks what they should be—the servants and not the masters of business."[16]

The currency system was similarly antiquated and unstable. Enough money was in circulation to take care of ordinary needs, but there was no way to expand the supply for the seasonal needs of farmers and industry or for stemming financial panics. And so banks often found themselves with either a surplus or a shortage of ready money.

The administration's answer to the banking and currency problems was the Federal Reserve System. Presented to Congress by Wilson in another ten-minute speech, it called for the creation of a central bank under public control. Another long and complicated battle ensued in Congress, but in the end Wilson got a law that satisfied him. He signed it in December 1913. What the law did in essence was give the nation a workable system of money reserves, establish an elastic currency system that could cope with varying needs for money and break down the concentration of credit in Wall Street. The Federal Reserve System, as modified from time to time, has exerted a powerful stablizing influence on banking and the operation of the national economy.

Wilson's third target was the control of business monopolies—the trusts, as they were called—that stifled competition in such industries as steel and oil. To this end, he pressed through Congress the Clayton Antitrust Act, which outlawed practices that restrained trade. Because the Clayton Act tried to define all possible forms of restraint of trade, many small businessmen complained that the law would lay them open to fines or jail terms for practices that they did not realize were in restraint of trade. To deal with those complaints, Wilson proposed the creation of a Federal Trade Commission that would oversee day-to-day activity in the business world and help businessmen to know what would be regarded as restraint of trade and what was acceptable competitive practice. Both of these measures became law in 1914.

These were the main achievements of Wilson's first year, but there were others. All in all, Wilson had accomplished more in a year than most presidents accomplish in a full term. As one journal put it after Wilson had been in office for two years:

> Aside from definite legislative achievements—tariff laws, currency reforms, trade commissions—Mr. Wilson has introduced one definite idea into American political life.

The Wilson family posed in 1913 in the yard of a home in New Hampshire where they spent part of the summer. From the left are Margaret, Ellen, Eleanor, Jessie and the president. (Library of Congress)

> Because of his career, American politics can never be precisely the same thing that it was before. This one idea is that of party leadership. . . . This, then, is President Wilson's great contribution to our political philosophy and practice. . . . He has given the office [of president] a new and high dignity; he has shown that it possesses greater power for usefulness than we had imagined; and certainly no President can have succeeded more completely than that.[17]

During all this activity in Wilson's first two years as president, the Wilson family saw both joy and tragedy. Two of the Wilson daughters were married in the White House. Jessie married Francis B. Sayre, a member of the faculty at Williams College, on November 25, 1913. (Sayre went on to teach at Harvard University and then to become a diplomat, serving as an assistant secretary of state and as an ambassador.) Eleanor married Secretary of the Treasury William G. McAdoo on May 7, 1914. The Sayres gave the president three grandchildren—Francis B. Sayre, Jr., Eleanor Axson Sayre and Woodrow Wilson Sayre—and the McAdoos two—Ellen Wilson McAdoo and Mary Faith McAdoo. The McAdoo marriage, however, did not last. McAdoo, the New York lawyer and businessman who had played a key role in Wilson's nomination, was 26 years older than Eleanor and a widower with six children at the time of the marriage. The McAdoos divorced in 1934, when McAdoo was a senator from California, and a year later he married a 26-year-old nurse. Eleanor did not marry again. Margaret Wilson never married.

But during the happy times of marrying daughters in the White House, it became increasingly apparent that Ellen Wilson was not well. She moved more and more slowly and became steadily weaker and paler. On March 1, 1914, she fell in her room at the White House. Her recovery from the effects of the heavy fall was very slow. She ate poorly and spent most of her time lying on a sofa or sitting outdoors in a wheelchair watching the gardeners work among her beloved flowers.

It was evident to Grayson and her other doctors that she had a serious kidney disease. Wilson, however, persisted in believing that she would get better. As late as June, he wrote to Mary Hulbert:

> The dear lady here is at last beginning to come uphill, and my reassurance lightens my heart immeasurably. For some time I was almost without hope: I thought, with leaden heart, that she was going to be an invalid, another victim of the too great burden that must be carried by the lady of the White House; but that fear, thank God, is past and she is coming along slowly but surely![18]

It was only a momentary improvement, however, and the "dear lady" grew steadily weaker. Wilson spent much of his time by her bed, holding her hand. That is what he was doing when she died, late in the afternoon of August 6. He looked up at Grayson and said, "Is it all over?"[19] Grayson nodded. Wilson went to a window overlooking the White House grounds, and Grayson heard him sob and say heavily, "Oh, my God, what am I to do?"[20]

He was devastated by his loss and had trouble carrying on his duties. To a friend he wrote:

I never understood before what a broken heart meant, and did for a man. It just means that he lives by the compulsion of necessity and duty only and has no other motive force. Business, the business of a great country that must be done and cannot wait, the problems that it would be deep unfaithfulness not to give my best powers to because a great people has trusted me, have been my salvation; but, oh! how hard, how desperately hard, it has been to face them, and to face them worthily! Every night finds me exhausted—dead in heart and body, weighed down with a leaden indifference and despair. . . .[21]

His daughters and his friends and his cousin Helen Bones, who came to live in the White House, tried to cheer him up. In the end it was Helen Bones, aided by Grayson, who indirectly brought joy to his life again. Ellen Wilson had told Grayson the day before her death that she wished Wilson would marry

Cary T. Grayson, Wilson's physician and close friend from the time Wilson became president, rides in Washington. His program of exercise, rest and diet greatly improved Wilson's health. Grayson was a naval officer, promoted to rear admiral by Wilson, who had also served as physician to Theodore Roosevelt and William Howard Taft during their terms as president.
(Library of Congress)

again and hoped Grayson would help him find another wife. Out riding with the president one day in the spring of 1915, Grayson bowed to an attractive woman he knew, and Wilson asked him, "Who was that beautiful lady?"[22] Grayson told him she was Edith Bolling Galt, widow of a jeweler in Washington.

Grayson, noting the president's interest, saw an opportunity to pursue Ellen Wilson's deathbed wishes. Moving subtly, he and Helen Bones went a few days later to Mrs. Galt's home in a White House car and invited her to join them in a ride. As he had hoped, the women became friends. One day, after they had been out for a walk, Helen Bones asked Mrs. Galt to join her for tea in the White House, assuring her that they would be by themselves because the president was out playing golf with Grayson. That was true, but as the women emerged from the White House elevator, they came face to face with the two golfers, who had just returned. Grayson suggested that the men might be invited to the tea. They were, and the president was charmed by his cousin's new friend. On April 7 Helen Bones persuaded the president to go on one of the automobile rides she had begun taking with Mrs. Galt. He did, and Mrs. Galt joined them afterward for dinner at the White House. Wilson was smitten and soon plunged into a spirited courtship of the lady. Courtship was made difficult by his prominent position. They took automobile rides, always with Helen Bones or someone else present, exchanged warm letters and talked on the telephone. In May he asked her to marry him. She had reservations because she had never been involved in public life and was not sure he really knew her. The courtship continued, growing more ardent, and in the fall she accepted his proposal. They announced their engagement on October 7 and were married in her small home at 1308 20th Street in Washington on December 18.

The marriage worked wonders for Wilson's spirits. Edith Wilson helped him with his work, acted as a sounding board for his ideas, played golf with him (she was as poor a golfer as he was), went on automobile rides with him and pleased him with her close attention to his needs and her good humor. He was "exceedingly, perfectly happy," he wrote to a friend; "Edith is a very wonderful person, really and truly."[23] And with his spirits restored, he rediscovered his enthusiasm for his work.

It was just as well, for there was plenty of it, mostly involving foreign affairs now. Relations with Mexico had become difficult after a Mexican general, Victoriano Huerta, overthrew the elected government in 1913 and established a military dictatorship. Wilson refused to recognize the new government and vowed to bring it down. He had to send the marines to Veracruz, Huerta's chief port, in the spring of 1914 in pursuit of that effort.

Huerta was finally defeated in the summer of 1914 and was succeeded by a group calling itself the Constitutionalists, led by Venustiano Carranza. Wilson recognized Carranza's government in 1915, but it was an unstable group, riven by internal disputes. One of Carranza's opponents, Pancho Villa, headed a rival movement in northern Mexico. Angered by Wilson's support of Carranza, Villa invaded the American town of Columbus, New Mexico, in March 1916, killing 19 residents and setting fire to buildings in the town.

Wilson responded by sending a force of 5,000 men into Mexico with orders to capture Villa. This "Punitive Expedition," commanded by Brigadier General John J. Pershing, pursued Villa for 11 months but failed to catch him. The episode further embittered American relations with Mexico, causing Carranza to complain repeatedly of American intervention in Mexican affairs. The dispute was teetering close to war when Wilson accepted Carranza's suggestion of an international commission to work out a settlement and quietly withdrew the Pershing expedition in January 1917.

An even darker cloud appeared on the horizon with the outbreak of war in Europe in 1914. The storm had been gathering for years as Germany, Austria-Hungary, France, Great Britain and Russia clashed repeatedly over territory and economic advantage. World War I, as it came to be known, had as its main combatants Britain, France and Russia (the Allies) on one side, Germany and Austria-Hungary (the Central Powers) on the other.

Although Wilson's sympathies lay with the Allies, he hoped the United States could remain neutral in the conflict. Neutrality, however, proved to be a difficult policy to maintain. Both the Allies, mainly the British, and the Central Powers, mainly the Germans, presented problems for the neutrality policy.

The British relied heavily on their powerful navy, which gave them dominance of the seas. They used the navy to intercept merchant ships carrying goods destined for Germany or likely to wind up there even if they were delivered first at a neutral port. Wilson tried to persuade both sides to accept the Declaration of London, an agreement on maritime warfare that had been drafted by an international conference five years before but never made part of international law. The British refused, objecting in particular to the Declaration's long "free list" of goods that could not be prevented from going to enemy territory and to its disapproval of the ancient principle of "continuous voyage," meaning that forbidden goods destined for an enemy could be seized even if they were going first to a neutral port. Wilson warned that the United States would persist in trying to claim what it believed to be its rights in wartime shipping.

The Germans wanted to keep goods from reaching the British, and early in 1915, they began a policy of merciless submarine warfare against all ships entering a war zone around the British Isles. At first, the Germans said they would try to spare American ships, but it was not always possible for a submarine commander sighting a ship through his periscope to identify its nationality or even to be sure it was a cargo vessel rather than a passenger ship. And so a German submarine would sometimes sink a passenger ship with Americans aboard. Each of these events provoked outrage in the United States. Then in May a U-boat (the English name for the German *Unterseeboot*, meaning undersea boat) sank the British liner *Lusitania*, causing the death of 1,198 people—124 of whom were Americans. This was war against civilians—and the howl of protest in the United States was deafening.

Wilson defused this crisis somewhat by persuading the Germans to say they would sink no passenger ships without giving warning first and arranging for the safety of the people aboard. But he had to respond to rising pressure at home for moves to improve the nation's military preparedness. It remained clear, however, that most Americans—even though they might favor more preparedness—wanted to stay out of the war.

It was in this turbulent situation that Wilson ran for reelection in 1916. The Republicans nominated Charles Evans Hughes, a justice of the Supreme Court who had earlier been governor of New York. Even though the Democrats campaigned on the strong slogan that Wilson had "kept us out of war," the election was extremely close: 9,129,606 votes for Wilson and 8,538,221 for Hughes. Wilson did not know until three days after the vote that his victory would be assured by California's electoral votes. With them, the tally in the electoral college was 277 to 254.

Although Wilson knew that he owed his reelection largely to his efforts to keep the nation out of the war, events conspired to make the task increasingly difficult. In January 1917, the Germans announced that their submarines would henceforth attack all ships, neutral and belligerent, in European waters. Wilson's response was to break off relations with Germany and to move to what he called "armed neutrality" by giving American merchant ships weapons to defend themselves against German submarines. Then, in February, Wilson got wind of what came to be known as the Zimmerman telegram—a message from Arthur Zimmerman, the German foreign minister, to the Mexicans inviting them into an alliance with Germany. If the United States entered the war, Mexico would join the war, too, against the United States, and would receive Texas, New Mexico and Arizona as a reward if Germany triumphed.

The news of the meddlesome Zimmerman telegram inflamed public opinion in the United States. Germany's all-out submarine warfare fanned the flames. In one day, March 18, U-boats sank three American merchantships without warning. Many newspapers and political leaders were declaring that the time had come to enter the war. Wilson at last agreed, swayed in part by the belief that American participation would hasten the end of the war and, in part, by the certainty that participation would guarantee the United States a seat at the peace table. Appearing before Congress on April 2, 1917, Wilson asked for a declaration of war against the Central Powers:

> With a profound sense of the solemn and even tragical character of the step I am taking and of the grave responsibilities which it involves, but in unhesitating obedience to what I deem my constitutional duty, I advise that the Congress declare the recent course of the Imperial German Government to be in fact nothing less than war against the government and people of the United States; that it formally accept the status of belligerent which has thus been

thrust upon it; and that it take immediate steps not only to put the country in a more thorough state of defense but also to exert all its power and employ all its resources to bring the Government of the German Empire to terms and end the war. . . .

The world must be made safe for democracy.[24]

The Senate passed the war resolution on April 4, the House on April 6. Wilson signed it on April 7. Neutrality was at an end.

Notes

1. Arthur Walworth, *Woodrow Wilson* (New York: W. W. Norton and Company, 1978), vol. 1, p. 263.
2. *The New York Times*, March 5, 1913, p. 2.
3. *The New York Times*, March 5, 1913, p. 2.
4. Irwin Hood Hoover, *Forty-two Years in the White House* (Boston: Houghton Mifflin, 1934), p. 244.
5. Josephus Daniels, *The Wilson Era, Years of Peace — 1910–1917* (Chapel Hill, N.C.: The University of North Carolina Press, 1944), p. 137.
6. Arthur S. Link, *Wilson: The New Freedom* (Princeton, N.J.: Princeton University Press, 1956), p. 80.
7. Arthur S. Link, ed.*Woodrow Wilson: A Profile* (New York: Hill and Wang, 1968), p. 93.
8. Link, *Woodrow Wilson: A Profile*, p. 93.
9. Cary T. Grayson, *Woodrow Wilson, An Intimate Memoir*, (New York: Holt, Rinehart and Winston, 1960), pp. 2–3.
10. Grayson, *Woodrow Wilson, An Intimate Memoir*, pp. x–xi.
11. Grayson, *Woodrow Wilson, An Intimate Memoir*, p. 12.
12. Walworth, *Woodrow Wilson*, vol. 1, p. 293.
13. Link, *Wilson: The New Freedom*, p. 180.
14. Walworth, *Woodrow Wilson*, vol. 1, p. 299.
15. John A. Garraty, *Woodrow Wilson* (Westport, Conn.: Greenwood Press, 1977), p. 84.
16. Link, *Wilson: The New Freedom*, p. 211.
17. *The World's Work*, March, 1915, p. 489.
18. Link, *Wilson: The New Freedom*, p. 461.
19. Link, *Wilson: The New Freedom*, p. 462.
20 Link, *Wilson: The New Freedom*, p. 462.

21. Link, *Wilson: The New Freedom*, p. 463.
22. Walworth, *Woodrow Wilson*, vol. 1, p. 426.
23. Walworth, *Woodrow Wilson*, vol. 1, p. 441.
24. *The New York Times*, April 3, 1917, p. 1.

THE WARTIME PRESIDENT
(1917–1918)

For a peace-minded president, leading the nation into a massive and technologically advanced war required a major change of direction. Wilson's move to improve the nation's preparedness had barely begun. An army of scarcely 100,000 men had to be greatly increased; to do so would require an enormous recruiting, training and supply program. Similarly, the navy and the merchant marine needed many more ships of all kinds, and crews to operate them. Industry and the transportation system had to be mobilized to focus their activities on the war effort.

Wilson made the change smoothly. Indeed, he seemed to take to the leadership of a warring nation as readily as he had taken charge at Princeton, as governor in New Jersey and in Washington immediately after his inauguration.

One of the first problems Wilson faced was how to obtain the men for the vast enlargement of the army. Volunteers presented themselves from all parts of the country. Theodore Roosevelt called at the White House on April 10, 1917, with an offer to raise a division and take it to France under his command.

But Wilson did not believe in a volunteer army. He sided with the view presented to him a few months earlier by General Hugh L. Scott, the army chief of staff, who said that "the only democratic method is for every man in his youth to become trained in order that he may render efficient service."[1] And so, calling on Congress to increase the army by half a million men, Wilson said they "should be chosen upon the principle of universal liability to service."[2] That meant a law setting up a draft system. The result was the Selective Service Act, adopted by Congress on April 28. It brought the National Guard into federal service and set up a system of local draft boards to bring into the army young men who were not involved in essential civilian services or war production. The first draft day was June 5, and ten million men between the ages of 21 and 30 registered with their draft boards. The draft provided nearly three million men for the armed forces during the war.

Although Wilson would have preferred not sending any American troops abroad until a million draftees had been trained, he yielded to Allied calls for a token force. In May he announced what he called an expeditionary force of about one army division would be sent to France as soon as possible. For its commander he reached past several senior generals to choose John J. Pershing, by now a major general, who had commanded the Punitive Expedition in Mexico.

The administration had hoped, in fact, that America's main contribution to the war could be in the form of weapons and supplies to the Allied troops. But Pershing, who went to France almost immediately after his appointment to sound out the situation, reported that the war would have to be won on the European battlefront and that the effort would require a large American force. Wilson accepted that judgment, and by the end of the war more than a million American soldiers were in France.

War is a costly business that is seldom included beforehand in a nation's budget. World War I was to cost the United States almost $36 billion. The question of how to raise that money provoked a battle of its own. Progressive members of both parties in Congress wanted to get a significant part of it from the income tax, placed particularly on the wealthier people, who were seen as best able to carry the burden. Conservatives argued for heavy borrowing and for sales taxes. Wilson sided with the progressives. Under pressure from the administration, Congress passed the War Revenue Act of 1917, which put the highest income tax at 67 percent. It also imposed a graduated tax on corporate profits above a certain level; the higher the profit, the higher the tax.

It was the highest tax level in the nation's history, but it was not enough. In May 1918, Wilson asked Congress to raise it higher. The Revenue Act of 1918 put the maximum income tax at 77 percent and the excess-profit tax at a maximum of 65 percent. Many people were bitter about the high taxes, and that bitterness was to be a factor in the national elections of 1920.

Even at these rates, taxes raised only about a third of the cost of the war, and the government had to resort to a series of bond issues that went by the name of Liberty Loans. There were five of them over a period of two years, and the public paid more than $21 billion to buy the bonds. Wilson, who was not a wealthy man, bought $10,000 worth of the bonds in the first issue and made war bonds his only investments throughout the war.

Manpower and financing only begin to indicate the complexity of the problems Wilson faced in shifting the nation's economy from peace to war. Wilson made a basic decision very early: He would not load the burdens of war onto the existing government departments (other than State, War and Navy), but instead would create new agencies to cope with the problems raised by the war. Among the agencies were the Committee on Public Information, headed by George Creel, and the War Industries Board, headed by Bernard Baruch. Wilson also appointed men who might be described as "czars" to deal with particularly crucial areas. Herbert Hoover (a Republican who was elected president 10 years after the war) became food administrator, and Henry Garfield was fuel administrator. Creel, Baruch, Hoover and Garfield—along with Secretary of War Newton D. Baker and Secretary of the Navy Josephus Daniels—formed what came to be known as the "War Cabinet," which met once a week to discuss war policies. The historian John A. Garraty has described the group's proceedings:

> The meetings were held in Wilson's study, overlooking the Potomac. After greeting his advisers, passing out cigars, and perhaps telling a funny story to break the tension, the President would clear his desk and get down to work. Each

Wilson and his second wife, Edith Bolling Galt, leave Constitution Hall in Washington. She was the widow of a Washington jeweler when Wilson met her in 1915 through a bit of maneuvering by Grayson, who had been asked by Ellen Wilson on her deathbed to encourage Wilson to marry again. Mrs. Galt and Wilson were married at her home in Washington near the end of that year. (Library of Congress)

member would raise his own particular problems, which all would discuss. Wilson served as coordinator; he kept the discussions orderly, absorbed information, and in the end made the decisions.[3]

Government people involved in the war became familiar with documents that, having been sent to the president for consideration, came back with "Okeh, W. W.," written on them in Wilson's hand. Edith Wilson later reported that someone asked Wilson why he did not use the more familiar "O.K." Wilson replied, "Because it is wrong," and suggested that the inquirer look it up in the dictionary. The inquirer did so and found that "okeh" is a Choctaw word meaning "It is so."[4] (The *Oxford English Dictionary* says, "The suggestion that they [the letters O.K.] represent the Choctaw *oke* 'it is' first appeared in 1885, and does not accord with the evidence.")[5]

Edith Wilson revealed something of the strain the wartime months put on her husband's health:

[During the war] there would come days when he was incapacitated by blinding headaches that no medicine could relieve. He would have to give up everything, and the only cure seemed to be sleep. . . . Sometimes this sleep would last five, six, or even eight hours. He would awaken refreshed and able at once to take up work and go on with renewed energy.[6]

America had been in the war only a few months before it became clear that the nation's railroads, already busy with the level of traffic that was normal in peacetime, could not cope efficiently with the added wartime demand for moving troops, food and military supplies. Finally, in December 1917, Wilson took possession of the railroads in the government's name and appointed Treasury Secretary William G. McAdoo to run them. The appointment gave Wilson some anguish, since he disapproved of giving government appointments to relatives and McAdoo was now his son-in-law. But McAdoo already had a government appointment, made before he married Eleanor Wilson. And since Wilson thought McAdoo was the best man to run the railroads, he gave McAdoo the job anyway. McAdoo acted vigorously to speed up the movement of war-related goods over the rails.

Fuel, which was mostly coal in those days, also presented a problem. It was quickly apparent that fuel supplies could not keep up with both civilian needs and the demands of the war industries. Wilson's advisers told him it would be necessary to cut down civilian fuel consumption by designating "heatless days" and by closing offices and factories from time to time. The president knew that such steps would be highly unpopular, but he took them anyway. As Wilson had predicted, there was a great outcry, but he stood firm. "It is extraordinary," he wrote to Bernard Baruch at the time, "how some people wince and cry out when they are a little bit hurt."[7]

Criticism came from a more troublesome source in January 1918. The Senate's Committee on Military Affairs, which had been monitoring the munitions program, decided that the gap between production goals and actual output was too great. Senator George Chamberlain of Oregon, chairman of the committee, made a speech in New York declaring that "the Military Establishment of America has fallen down" and "has almost stopped functioning . . . because of inefficiency in every bureau and in every department of the Government."[8] Conservative Republicans set up a cry for the creation of a War Cabinet, consisting of members of both parties, to take over control of the war.

Wilson thought the criticism was unjustified, but he saw in it a chance to tighten his own control over the war effort. At his urging, Senator Lee Overman of North Carolina introduced a bill that would give the president stronger power to organize and direct government agencies in the conduct of the war. Although opponents in Congress denounced the bill as making the president a dictator, it passed. As the historian Frederick L. Paxson later wrote, "Few statutes have in so few words surrendered so much; and none has vested more discretion in the President."[9]

Wilson used his discretion to vest more power in the War Industries Board, which he had created in the summer of 1917 to supervise war production and control the flow of raw materials. With his new power, Wilson made the board an independent body and named Bernard Baruch as its chairman. Baruch, a man with a strong hand and a wide acquaintance among businessmen, quickly brought order and efficiency to war production.

Although the war made Wilson work longer hours and put him under great strain, he still found time for recreation. He and Grayson continued to play golf. Unwilling to take his regular Sunday automobile ride because Sunday had been declared a "gasless day" to help conserve fuel for the war effort, he rode instead in a fringed surrey drawn by two horses; the ever-present Secret Service detail accompanied him on bicycles. He continued to go regularly to the theater—a lifelong love of his. He once said to his daughter Eleanor, "I shall never grow up. I would rather see poor acting than not go to a play when I have a chance."[10] Edmund W. Starling, a Secret Service agent who was almost constantly with Wilson in public as a member of the White House detail, wrote years later:

> Looking back on it now I realize that the President got more genuine recreation from the theatre than he did from anything else. It entirely relaxed his mind, and it is worth

noting that he preferred musical comedies and good vaudeville to serious dramatic works. He was not interested in anything which would require the use of his mind.[11]

Wilson still took rides on the Potomac in the *Mayflower*. On these trips he liked to study the charts of the waterways and sail into places that looked interesting. In such a place he would pass the time with the fishermen and sometimes buy fish from them for his lunch. He continued to go to baseball games. After one of them, confronting a package of problems brought in by the fuel administrator, he said, "Hang it all, Garfield, I have just been to a ball game and I wish I could say three strikes and out to this job."[12] Often in the evening he and Edith Wilson would listen to opera music played on an electric self-playing piano.

Gradually, the weight of American troops, ships and supplies made itself felt in the war. The U-boats were swept from the seas and the troops of the Central Powers began to buckle on land. One by one, the allies of the Germans surrendered—Bulgaria first, followed by Turkey and Austria-Hungary. Kaiser Wilhelm II, the German emperor, fled into exile in Holland, and two days later—November 11, 1918—the government that succeeded him agreed to an armistice. Wilson was now able to turn to what he regarded as the crucial task of shaping a peace.

When addressing Congress in January of 1918, Wilson had laid the framework for the peace he envisioned. His Fourteen Points, as the plan came to be known, called for freedom of the seas and a general reduction of armaments and, above all, for "a general association of nations"[13] that would seek to keep the world at peace. In achieving this vision of peace, Wilson was determined to take a strong personal hand.

Notes

1. Arthur Walworth, *Woodrow Wilson* (New York: W. W. Norton and Company, 1978), vol. 2, p. 105.
2. Walworth, *Woodrow Wilson*, vol. 2, p. 105.
3. John A. Garraty, *Woodrow Wilson* (Westport, Conn.: Greenwood Press, 1977), pp. 119–120.
4. Edith Bolling Wilson, *My Memoir* (New York: The Bobbs-Merrill Company, 1939), p. 145.

5. *The Oxford English Dictionary* (New York: Oxford University Press, 1933), Supplement, p. 82.
6. Edith Bolling Wilson, *My Memoir*, p. 116.
7. Walworth, *Woodrow Wilson*, vol. 2, p. 159.
8. Arthur S. Link, *Woodrow Wilson: A Brief Biography* (Cleveland: The World Publishing Company, 1963), p. 123.
9. Frederic L. Paxson, *America at War* (Boston: Houghton Mifflin, 1939), pp. 224–225.
10. Eleanor Wilson McAdoo, *The Woodrow Wilsons* (New York: Macmillan, 1937), p. 190.
11. Edmund W. Starling, *Starling of the White House* (New York: Simon and Schuster, 1946), pp. 104–105.
12. Walworth, *Woodrow Wilson*, vol. 2, p. 165.
13. *The New York Times*, January 9, 1918, p. 1.

THE PEACEMAKING PRESIDENT (1918–1921)

With the war over, the peace-minded president was able to turn to the task that absorbed him most—drafting a treaty that would formally end the war on terms that he regarded as fair and providing an international body (to be called the League of Nations) that would seek to prevent future wars. It turned out to be his hardest task and ultimately his greatest short-term failure. The tragic saga prompted the historian Thomas A. Bailey to write that one of the great ironies of history is that "the peace-loving President Wilson ... attained far greater success in making war than in making peace."[1]

The basic problem Wilson faced was that his British and French allies, who had borne most of the burden of lost lives, bloodshed and damage in the war, were out to see that Germany was punished. They wanted reparations—territory and money from the Germans to compensate in part for the losses. Wilson was out for a peace based on high principles: disarmament, freedom of the seas, no reparations, the right of subject peoples to determine their own fate and, above all, an international body to preserve peace. As he had said in a famous speech to the Senate shortly before the United States entered the war, it "must be a peace without victory. . . . Victory would mean peace forced upon the loser, a victor's terms imposed upon the vanquished."[2]

But that was exactly what the British and the French sought: a victor's terms imposed upon the vanquished. That was why Wilson decided to go himself to the peace conference in Paris in an effort to lead the talks in what he saw as the right direction. A few of his associates advised him against going, and urged him to delegate the duty to someone else. Herbert Hoover was one of them. Joseph Tumulty, his secretary and adviser on political matters, said that problems at home would suffer in the president's absence and that the Republicans would gain accordingly. Robert Lansing, the secretary of state, advised Wilson that he would have much more influence on the peace conference if he stayed home, preaching his high principles and building up support for the League of Nations, than if he went to Paris and got into the thick of the battle. (Lansing wrote that Wilson's expression became harsh and stubborn when he heard this advice. "He said nothing, but looked volumes.")[3] But Wilson had made up his mind, and he left for Europe aboard the *George Washington* on December 4, 1918.

Wilson had already suffered a serious defeat and therefore arrived in Paris at a disadvantage. In October, he had drafted a message that he wanted to release to the American people, calling on them to elect a Democratic Congress. Don't do it, Tumulty said—it will fan the partisan fires. Edith Wilson, when he read the message to her, said, "I would not send it out. It is not a dignified thing to do."[4] But the next day, he did it. "If you have approved of my leadership and wish me to continue to be your unembarrassed spokesman in affairs at home and abroad," he said, "I earnestly beg that you will express yourself unmistakably to that effect by returning a Democratic majority to both the Senate and the House of Representatives."[5]

Republican leaders, including former presidents Roosevelt and Taft, jumped on this appeal with glee. It was an insult, they said, to patriotic Republicans who had supported Wilson's conduct of the war. And on election day, November 5, the voters gave the Republicans control of both houses of Congress. An unusual coalition of voting groups brought about the result: blacks who had come north for war work and voted for the party that had freed the slaves at the end of the Civil War; women (who could vote in only 15 states in 1918—and only in state and local elections) because they thought Southern Democrats in the Senate had blocked the constitutional amendment giving women the vote in all elections; business people who saw themselves as hurt by the New Freedom and the war restrictions; ethnic Germans who were bitter about the war against their former country, and people of Irish descent who hated the British; and wealthy voters who resented the high taxes the war had brought.

The election of a Republican Congress, Wilson had said, would be "interpretive on the other side of the water as a repudiation of my leadership."[6] And now that was the condition in which he departed for Europe. Worse, he would now have to press the peace treaty on a Senate controlled by Republicans, several of whom had already voiced doubts about American participation in an international peacekeeping organization.

For the moment, however, it was all cheers. As the *George Washington* drew near the French coast early in the morning of December 13, nine battleships greeted the president with a 21-gun salute. Shore batteries did the same. Military bands atop the cliffs bordering the channel played the American and French national anthems. French and American troops presented arms as the president came ashore to be greeted by the mayor of Brest. Above the road leading to the railroad station, where the president and his party would enter the private train of French President Poincaré, hung banners saying "Hail the Champion of the Rights of Man. Honor to the Apostle of International Justice. Honor and Welcome to the Founder of the Society of Nations."[7] As the train proceeded to Paris, people stood beside the tracks and shouted greetings to the president. In Paris, a huge crowd packed the streets and cheered "Vive Wilson" as the two presidents rode by in a carriage drawn by two horses. "No one ever had such cheers," the journalist William Bolitho wrote. "Wilson heard from his carriage something . . . superhuman."[8]

A few days later, the president went to England, where immense crowds cheered him as he rode through the streets with King George V. And then it was Italy and another ceremonial welcome and more cheering throngs.

But at last it was time to get down to business. And business at a peace conference involving 32 nations (all that had declared war on Germany) was complicated and slow-moving.

Each nation had a large number of official delegates, and each delegation brought along a large number of experts to provide advice on matters that would or might come up. And so, although the final decisions were made by what came to be known as the Council of Four and the Big Four—Wilson, Prime Minister David Lloyd George of Great Britain, Premier Georges Clemenceau of France and Premier Vittorio Orlando of Italy—the proceedings involved countless formal meetings, behind-the-scenes conferences and social gatherings.

It was not easy work. Lloyd George, Clemenceau and Orlando were determined to punish Germany by taking money and land and to disarm the Germans so that they could not threaten Europe again. Wilson's prime goal was to make the establishment of the League of Nations a key part of the peace treaty. The differences made for conflict and hard bargaining. Lloyd George illustrated their force when, talking about Wilson's call for freedom of the seas, he said to Colonel House:

> I could not accept the principle of Freedom of the Seas. It's no good saying I accept the principle. It would only mean that in a week's time a new Prime Minister would be here who would say that he could not accept this principle. The English people will not look at it.[9]

In February 1919, Wilson returned to Washington briefly for the concluding sessions of the Democratic 65th Congress, which would be succeeded in March by the Republican Congress elected the previous November. He left the American side of the peace negotiations in charge of his longtime intimate adviser Edward House. Although House was a man of few words who preferred to do his work behind the scenes, he had a large ego and seemed to think he knew more about peacemaking than Wilson did. He yielded ground on several points that Wilson had firmly defended. Wilson was furious. "House has given away everything I had won before we left Paris," he told his wife. "He has compromised on every side, and so I will have to start all over again and this time it will be harder, as he has given the impression that my delegates are not in sympathy with me."[10] The episode led to a break between Wilson and House that was not repaired in Wilson's lifetime.

Edward M. House, the man on the right, was one of Wilson's closest advisers during much of the Wilson administration. Texas, where he began his political career, had made him an honorary colonel, and he was usually known as Colonel House. His companion here is Sir Robert Borden, formerly prime minister of Great Britain. (Library of Congress)

No cheering throngs greeted the president when he returned to Paris. The people had thought the issues would be settled by this time, but the conference still dragged on. At one point, in April, the strain on Wilson brought him down with what was described as the flu. It was probably another cardiovascular problem as well, for he seemed to be a changed man when he resumed work. Ike Hoover describes the change:

> Even while lying in bed he manifested peculiarities, one of which was to limit the use of all the automobiles to strictly official purposes, when previously he had been so liberal in his suggestions that his immediate party should have the benefit of this possible diversion, in view of the long hours we were working. When he got back on the job, his peculiar ideas were even more pronounced. He now became obsessed with the idea that every French employee about the place was a spy for the French Government. Nothing we could say could disabuse his mind of this thought. He insisted they all understood English, when,

The Council of Four, also known as the Big Four, meets informally during the peace conference in Paris following World War I. From the left they are British prime minister David Lloyd George, Italian premier Vittorio Orlando, French premier Georges Clemenceau and Wilson. They made major decisions in shaping the Treaty of Versailles. (Library of Congress)

as a matter of fact, there was just one of them among the
two dozen or more who understood a single word of English. About this time he also acquired the peculiar notion
that he was personally responsible for all the property in
the furnished palace he was occupying. He raised quite a
fuss on two occasions when he noticed articles of furniture
had been removed. Upon investigation—for no one else
had noticed the change—it was learned that the custodian
of the property for the French owner had seen fit to do a
little rearranging. Coming from the President, whom we
all knew so well, these were funny things, and we could
but surmise that something queer was happening in his
mind.[11]

In the end, the peace conference settled on a considerably
more punitive treaty than Wilson had hoped for. It virtually
disarmed Germany and called for substantial reparations. The
amount Germany would have to pay was left open, whereas
Wilson had argued for a limit on it. The treaty also restored
the independence of Belgium, overrun by the Germans early
in the war; put the German colonies under the control of the
League of Nations; gave most of West Prussia to Poland, and
disposed of other parts of the German empire. But Wilson got
in the treaty the prize that he wanted most: the Covenant, as
he called it, establishing the League of Nations. The treaty was
signed at Versailles on June 28, 1919, and Wilson promptly
boarded the *George Washington* to return home and present
the treaty to the Senate.

He did that on July 10, telling the senators that the League
of Nations represented the hopes of mankind. "Dare we reject
it and break the heart of the world?"[12]

Yes, a number of people did dare to reject it. Most of the
Republicans in the Senate, reflecting the historic distaste of
Americans for foreign involvements, would approve membership in the League only if Wilson would accept "reservations"
to the treaty. The reservationists focused on Articles X and XI
of the Covenant. Those articles committed members of the
League to protect the independence of any member threatened
by external aggression and to "take any action that may be
deemed wise and effectual to safeguard the peace of nations."[13]
That meant, said the reservationists, a possible commitment
of American troops in a foreign war. A reservation declaring

that America would make its own decisions in such situations was necessary. Senator Henry Cabot Lodge of Massachusetts, an implacable foe of the League and no admirer of Wilson, led the battle for reservations.

Wilson would not compromise. He worked hard to influence individual senators to accept the Covenant as it was drafted. But he could see by the middle of August that he was losing ground, and he decided then to take his case to the people. When they heard his message, he believed, they would support him, and the weight of their support would move the Senate. And so, on September 3, he started his fateful trip across the country to deliver the message personally in city after city.

His message was that America had become a world leader and must face up to that role. The responsible way to do so, he said was through the League of Nations. And the keystone of the League was Article X of the Covenant. As he put it in Reno, Nevada:

> Article X is the heart of the enterprise. Article X is the test of the honor and courage and endurance of the world. Article X says that every member of the League . . . solemnly engages to respect and preserve as against external aggression the territorial integrity and existing political independence of the other members of the League. If you do that, you have absolutely stopped ambitious and aggressive war. . . . As against external aggression, as against ambition, as against the desire to dominate from without, we all stand together in a common pledge, and that pledge is essential to the peace of the world.[14]

And what was more vital to the national interest of the United States than the preservation of peace? Remarking on the number of children he saw in the crowds around his train, he said:

> I know that if by any chance we should not win this great fight for the League of Nations it would be their death warrant. They belong to the generation which would have to fight the final war, and in that final war there would not be merely seven and a half million men slain. The very existence of civilization would be in the balance.[15]

It was moving oratory by a superb orator. The crowds responded to it with enthusiasm. It appeared that Wilson might be right in his belief that he could move the people and they could move the Senate. And then came the tragic night in Pueblo, Colorado. The Secret Service man Edmund Starling, who was with the president, described the scene:

> While he spoke I stood close behind him, afraid he might collapse at any moment. Much of his speech was mumbled; he mouthed certain words as though he had never spoken them before. There were long pauses. He had difficulty following the trend of his thought. It was a travesty of his usual brilliant delivery and fine logic. His voice was weak, and every phrase was an effort for his whole body. Once he wept. . . .[16]

The trip was canceled, and the special train hastened back to Washington with the stricken president. And then, on the morning of October 2, came the massive stroke, with the result that, as Hoover put it, "never afterwards was he more than a shadow of his former self."[17] A stroke is a circulatory mishap in the brain. In Wilson's case it was a clot in an artery of his head; the clot impaired the circulation of blood to his brain. The result, according to a physician who has studied the records of Wilson's illnesses, was "a complete paralysis of the left side of his body, a loss of sensation on that side, and a left homonymous hemianopia—a loss of vision in the left half fields of both eyes."[18]

Ike Hoover, and Edith Wilson later, gave differing accounts of the attack. Hoover says:

> At exactly ten minutes before nine o'clock on this memorable day (I noted the time in writing the same day) my telephone on the desk in the Usher's Room at the White House rang and Mrs. Wilson's voice said, "Please get Doctor Grayson, the President is very sick." The telephone used was a private one that did not go through the general telephone switchboard. Mrs. Wilson had come all the way out to the end of the upper hall to use this particular telephone instead of the regular one in their bedroom. I reasoned at the time that it was done to avoid publicity, for there had been talk about the operators of the

switchboard listening in and disseminating information they picked up.[19]

Late in the afternoon, Hoover was called to the president's bedroom to help rearrange furniture. In his account of the scene he wrote:

> The President lay stretched out on the large Lincoln bed. He looked as if he were dead. There was not a sign of life. His face had a long cut about the temple from which the signs of blood were still evident. His nose also bore a long cut lengthwise. . . .
> Soon after, I made confidential inquiry as to how and when it all happened. I was told—and know it to be right—that he had gone to the bathroom upon arising in the morning and was sitting on the stool when the affliction overcame him; that he tumbled to the floor, striking his head on the sharp plumbing of the bathtub as he fell; Mrs. Wilson, hearing groans from the bathroom, went in and found him in an unconscious condition. She dragged him to the bed in the room adjoining and came out into the hall to call over the telephone for the doctor.[20]

Edith Wilson, in her memoir, says of the injuries described in the "rather remarkable account" by Hoover that "Dr. Grayson and I did not see these things."[21] According to her account, at the moment of the stroke Wilson slid to the floor and lay unconscious but uninjured. In considering the difference in the two accounts, one should bear in mind that Mrs. Wilson was fiercely protective of her husband's reputation, then and for the four remaining decades of her life. She spoke later of her determination that neither the public nor her husband should know how sick he really was.

In fact, he was very sick. Besides his left-side paralysis and his impaired vision, he had difficulty speaking. He was bedridden until the end of October, and then he could not support himself either sitting or standing. He had to be moved about in a wheelchair fitted with braces. Not until after Christmas was he able to stand and walk a few steps with the aid of a cane.

Grayson knew full well how sick his patient was. He and the other doctors who had seen the president decided two days after the stroke to make a full statement of Wilson's condition. They held back, however, in deference to Mrs. Wilson's wishes.

And so, as one writer has put it, there began "with the silent assent of some, with the active maneuvering of others, such a cover-up as American history had not known before."[22] Grayson's daily bulletins and Tumulty's meetings with reporters gave no hint of the seriousness of the president's condition. He was suffering, they said, from the effects of overwork and exhaustion. The public was given the impression that the government was carrying on as usual.

But it was not. Messages from members of the cabinet and other high government officials came to the White House and received no reply. Bills passed by Congress became law without the president's signature—an outcome made possible by the provision in the Constitution giving the president ten days to approve or veto a bill before it becomes law without his signature. Sometimes a matter that absolutely required action by the president resulted in a message written by Tumulty over the president's name or a statement by Mrs. Wilson conveying what she said was the president's decision. If he had to sign something, Mrs. Wilson held his hand and guided it.

It was not that Wilson was incapable of understanding things. His mind was clear, although he tired quickly in trying to dictate messages or to deal with the few problems Mrs. Wilson brought to him. His limitations were physical. He probably could have handled more matters than he did, if they had come to him. But these items did not come because Mrs. Wilson, concerned that work would make him worse, kept them from him.

With the true picture concealed from the public, rumors began to circulate. One of them was that the president's mind was blank and that all he could do was recite limericks. This story apparently originated from Grayson's report to some associates of an incident a few days after Wilson's stroke. The president, still too weak to feed himself, had raised a finger to stop Mrs. Wilson as she held a spoon to his lips and had then motioned to Grayson to come close. Grayson bent over the bed and heard the stricken man say, "A wonderful bird is the pelican; his bill will hold more than his bellican. He can take in his beak enough food for a week. I wonder how in the hell-he-can."[23] In fact, Wilson had been a reciter of limericks all his life, and this was one of his favorites.

The concern about how capable Wilson was and who was actually running the government extended to Congress. Senator Albert B. Fall of New Mexico, a Republican and Wilson foe, wanted some proof that the president was able to function. Fall got himself appointed to a committee of two charged to visit the stricken leader, ostensibly to ask him about a crisis that had arisen because Mexico had kidnapped an American consular agent, William Jenkins. The other member of the committee was Senator Gilbert M. Hitchcock of Nebraska, a Democrat and Wilson supporter.

On the appointed day, early in December, Fall and Hitchcock arrived at the White House and were shown into the president's bedroom. The stage had been carefully set. The president was covered by blankets, with only his face and his good right arm visible. A copy of a Senate report on the Mexican situation was in place on a table to his right, where he could pick it up. Mrs. Wilson remained nearby, taking notes. Wilson shook hands with Fall, picked up the report at an appropriate time and talked lucidly with the senators for 40 minutes. At the end, Fall bent over the bed and took Wilson's right hand again. "Mr. President, I am praying for you," he said. Wilson replied, with a chuckle, "Which way, Senator?"[24] Outside, Fall told reporters that the president "seemed to me to be in excellent trim, both mentally and physically."[25] Hitchcock had already said much the same thing, and the opinion of the two senators silenced voices in Congress that had been agitating for some move to replace Wilson, at least temporarily.

Gradually, the patient improved to the point where he could be somewhat more active. A daily routine developed, described by Chief Usher Hoover:

> The usual routine for weeks and weeks, in fact practically to the end, was for him to be taken from his bed about ten o'clock, placed in the [rolling] chair, and rolled to the south grounds; or, in bad weather, to the porch or some other room. The last year of his stay saw him in the East Room every day at twelve o'clock to look at a motion picture. We scoured the country that he might have a different picture each day. He would return to his bedroom at one o'clock,

Henry Cabot Lodge, Republican senator from Massachusetts, stands on the steps of the Senate building. As chairman of the Senate Committee on Foreign Relations, he led the successful battle against approval by the United States of the Versailles treaty, mainly because it would take the nation into the League of Nations—a new international peacekeeping body created largely at Wilson's insistence—without what Lodge regarded as adequate safeguards of American independence. (Library of Congress)

and be placed back in bed, where he would remain until the next morning.[26]

Meanwhile, the battle over the peace treaty continued in the Senate. Senator Lodge had brought the treaty out of the Committee on Foreign Relations and to the full Senate in November with 14 reservations. Hitchcock visited the president to discuss them. Grayson was present, looking after his patient as always. Wilson said, according to Grayson, "I consider it [the move to add reservations] a nullification of the Treaty and utterly impossible."[27] Several of his associates advised him to give some ground on the issue, but he refused. Even Mrs. Wilson urged him to yield. Later she described the scene:

> He turned his head on the pillow and stretching out his hand to take mine answered in a voice I shall never forget: "Little girl, don't you desert me; that I cannot stand. Can't you see that I have no moral right to accept any change in a paper I have signed without giving every other signatory, even the Germans, the right to do the same thing? It is not *I* that will not accept; it is the Nation's honour that is at stake. . . . Better a thousand times to go down fighting than to dip your colours to dishonourable compromise."[29]

It was a stalemate. In the end, when the Senate voted in March 1920, a majority favored the treaty, but that was not enough. Approval required a two-thirds vote. The other participants in the war approved the treaty, but in the United States it was dead, and the League of Nations did its work without American participation. Congress later passed a resolution declaring the war with Germany at an end. Wilson vetoed it. Not until 1921, after Wilson had left office, did a similar resolution become law.

Although Wilson was defeated, he continued to fight for his vision. He even let it be known that he would consider running for a third term so that he could carry on the fight. His friends were appalled at the thought. Grayson went to see Robert W. Woolley, a prominent delegate to the Democratic nominating convention in San Francisco, to emphasize that Wilson was not up to it. According to Woolley, Grayson said:

He [Wilson] still believes that it is possible to persuade the country to join the League without the Lodge reservations and he says that he would gladly resign when that has been accomplished. He couldn't survive the campaign. He is permanently incapacitated and gradually weakening mentally. At times by sheer grit he pulls himself together, keeps himself in good spirits for a week or ten days, transacts business through Tumulty, and even seems to improve. Then he slumps and turns so morose that it distresses me to be near him. We must take no chances in San Francisco.[29]

The delegates did not take any chances. Although Wilson's picture hung in the convention hall and the delegates cheered every mention of his name, they nominated Governor James M. Cox of Ohio. The nominee for vice president was a young man from New York who had served in the Wilson administration as assistant secretary of the navy—Franklin D. Roosevelt, who 12 years later would be the first Democrat after Wilson to be elected president.

The Republicans nominated Senator Warren G. Harding of Ohio for president and Calvin Coolidge, governor of Massachusetts, for vice president. With the country scrambling to get back to normal living after the distortions of the war, the Republicans campaigned on the theme of a "return to normalcy." They won the presidency handily and again carried both houses of Congress. It was clear that they would make no move to take the United States into the League of Nations. It may have been some consolation to Wilson that in December 1920, he was awarded the Nobel Peace Prize because of his efforts for the Versailles treaty and the League, but he had lost the main battle.

His term would end in March, 1921. He and Edith had already drawn up a chart rating places where they might live in retirement. It listed Baltimore, Washington, Richmond, Boston and New York, grading each of them under the headings of Climate, Friends, Opportunities, Freedom, Amusements and Libraries. In the end, they decided to stay in Washington. They had an architect draw up plans for houses they could build; Edith looked at houses in and near the District of Columbia, and finally they bought a large brick house at 2340 S Street, N.W., in Washington.

On March 1, 1921, Wilson met with his cabinet for the last time. One of the members asked what he would do in retirement, and he replied, "I am going to try to teach ex-Presidents how to behave."[30]

Notes

1. John A. Garraty, *Woodrow Wilson* (Westport, Conn.: Greenwood Press, 1977), p. 118.
2. *The New York Times*, January 23, 1917, p. 1.
3. Arthur Walworth, *Woodrow Wilson* (New York: W. W. Norton and Company, 1978), vol. 2, p. 206.
4. Walworth, *Woodrow Wilson*, vol. 2, p. 202.
5. *The New York Times*, October 26, 1918, p. 1.
6. *The New York Times*, October 26, 1918, p. 1.
7. Gene Smith, *When The Cheering Stopped* (New York: William Morrow and Company, 1964), p. 37.
8. Smith., *When The Cheering Stopped*, p.39.
9. Garraty, *Woodrow Wilson*, p. 136.
10. Arthur S. Link, *Woodrow Wilson: A Brief Biography* (Cleveland: The World Publishing Company, 1963), p. 146.
11. Irwin Hood Hoover, *Forty-two Years in the White House* (Boston: Houghton Mifflin, 1934), p. 98.
12. Link, *Woodrow Wilson: A Brief Biography*, p. 160.
13. Alden Hatch, *Woodrow Wilson* (New York: Henry Holt and Company, 1957), p. 253.
14. Link, *Woodrow Wilson: A Brief Biography*, pp. 164–165.
15. Link, *Woodrow Wilson: A Brief Biography*, p. 165.
16. Edmund W. Starling, *Starling of the White House* (New York: Simon and Schuster, 1946), pp. 151–152.
17. Hoover, *Forty-two Years in the White House*, p. 95.
18. Edwin A. Weinstein, *Woodrow Wilson: A Medical and Psychological Biography* (Princeton, N.J.: Princeton University Press, 1981), p. 357.
19. Hoover, *Forty-two Years in the White House*, p. 100.
20. Hoover, *Forty-two Years in the White House*, p. 102.
21. Edith Bolling Wilson, *My Memoir* (New York: The Bobbs-Merrill Company, 1938), p. 288.
22. August Heckscher, *Woodrow Wilson* (New York: Charles Scribner's Sons, 1991), p. 613.
23. Smith, *When the Cheering Stopped*, p. 111.

24. Smith, *When the Cheering Stopped*, p. 134.
25. *The New York Times,* December 6, 1919, p. 2.
26. Hoover, *Forty-two Years in the White House,* pp. 107–108.
27. Weinstein, *Woodrow Wilson: A Medical and Psychological Biography*, p. 361.
28. Edith Bolling Wilson, *My Memoir*, pp. 296–297.
29. Walworth, *Woodrow Wilson*, vol. 2, p. 400.
30. Smith, *When the Cheering Stopped*, p. 179.

EPILOGUE:

(1921–1924)

Wilson's method of teaching ex-presidents how to behave turned out to be by example rather than by word. He had numerous chances to earn money by writing: a history of the peace negotiations in Paris (for $150,000, a princely sum in those days), prefaces for books, book reviews, a series of monthly articles for the *Ladies' Home Journal* (at $5,000 per article) and his memoirs. He could have used the money—the Wilsons were not particularly well off and, in fact, had help from friends in buying the S Street house—but he turned down all the offers. "What I have done and stood for is of record," he said, "and any consequent interpretation or explanation that I might make would not affect the event, and would not be a contribution to history."[1]

He was similarly scrupulous about accepting business for the law firm that he formed with Bainbridge Colby, who had been secretary of state in Wilson's last year as president. Clients who hoped to benefit from the impact of having the ex-president as their lawyer offered fat fees, but Wilson turned them down. "Day after day," Colby said to Edith Wilson after a few months of this, "I sit in my office and see a procession walk through—thousands and thousands of dollars—and not one to put in our pockets." But, he added, it "is a sublime position on the part of your husband."[2] Struggling to maintain luxurious offices in New York and Washington while turning away large fees, the partners agreed in the fall of 1922 to dissolve the firm.

On Wilson's retirement from the presidency in 1921, he and his wife moved into this house at 2340 S Street in northwest Washington, D.C. The house appears here as it looked at about the time when the Wilsons bought it. They added a driveway and garage on the right side. The house, now owned by the National Trust for Historic Preservation, is open to visitors, who see it just as it looked when the Wilsons lived there. (Library of Congress)

Wilson did try to do some writing, but on his own terms rather than in response to offers of money. One plan was to turn at last to a work that he had planned at Princeton—a book on the philosophy of politics. He wrote a dedication to his wife, and that was as far as he got with the book. In 1923, he assembled, dictating to Edith, an essay called "The Road Away from Revolution." Although the *Atlantic Monthly* published it and paid him $200 for it, it was a pale effort compared to his earlier writing.

Mostly he lived the quiet life of an unwell man in retirement. The usual routine began with breakfast in his bedroom on the third floor. As he ate, Mrs. Wilson read him items from the newspapers. After breakfast, he walked a short distance to the elevator and rode to the ground floor. There, in the cozy library, he went over some of the many letters that came in every day. They had been sorted by John Bolling (Edith's brother, who served as Wilson's secretary and also kept a daily journal of activities in the house), and to those that Bolling thought needed personal replies from the ex-president, Wilson would dictate a response. That task done, he turned to the daily exercise urged on him by Grayson. It consisted of several walking trips back and forth in the rather wide entrance hallway. It was difficult work, with his uncooperative left leg, and he used a cane, which he often called his third leg.

Then it was back to the third floor, where he shaved himself—another difficult task, given his disabilities, but he insisted on doing it himself. Usually he had lunch in his bedroom with Edith. Sometimes during the afternoon he would see a visitor. Visitors were carefully screened by Edith, and she usually dealt with most of them herself, allowing only old friends to spend some time with Wilson. An afternoon automobile ride was standard. At first the car was a Pierce Arrow that Wilson had bought from the White House fleet, and then it was an elegant Rolls Royce given to him by some of his friends.

Returning from the ride, he would have dinner in the library. After dinner, Edith read to him—novels, detective stories and magazine articles. Occasionally they watched a movie in the house or went out to a vaudeville show. Less often, they went to a play or to a baseball game at Griffith Stadium, home of the Washington Senators of the American League.

In the fall of 1923, he had a visit from Bernard Baruch's daughter Belle, who was working with groups favoring American membership in the League of Nations. She asked him to go on the radio the night before Armistice Day to promote the cause. He disliked the radio, which, at that time, was quite a new medium, but for the League and in memory of the armistice he agreed to make a talk. He struggled to write the talk and he struggled in giving it. Edith had to prompt him from time to time. But millions of people heard him and were touched.

On Armistice Day, thousands of people came to stand in front of the house in tribute to the ex-president. That afternoon, accompanied by Senator Carter Glass of Virginia, Wilson came out onto the front steps, where the crowd greeted him with applause and cheers. Glass read a short speech and then Wilson gave a short talk about the war and the armistice. Finishing it, he turned to go back into the house, helped by Hubert Thompson, a member of the Federal Trade Commission who had been one of Wilson's students at Princeton. The noise from the cheering crowd and from a band playing the hymn "How Firm a Foundation" was tremendous. Wilson stopped and said to Thompson, "Stop the band. I have something more to say."[3] Thompson waved his arms, and the crowd fell silent. Wilson said, speaking more vigorously than he had in months:

> Just one word more. I cannot refrain from saying it. I am not one that has the least anxiety about the triumph of the principles I have stood for. I have seen fools resist Providence before, and I have seen their destruction, as will come upon these again, utter destruction and contempt. That we shall prevail is as sure as that God reigns. Thank you.[4]

It was his last public utterance. He carried on through December and January, seeing occasional visitors and pressing still his message that America must join the League of Nations. But his health, which had improved somewhat since his retirement, began to decline. Grayson later gave this report:

> After he took up residence in S Street until the summer of 1923, there was a slow improvement in his condition, no marked change from week to week, but a gratifying change when his case was reviewed over the period of months. The chart showed a general improvement. The muscles of the affected left side grew stronger. . . . He was game and tried to take advantage of each upward step. There was, however, a general arteriosclerosis, which, of course, made final recovery impossible.
>
> In the autumn of 1923, his good eye began to fail; there were minute hemorrhages in the retina. Though he kept his courage and was frequently as cheerful as he had ever

Wilson, in broken health because of a stroke he suffered in 1919, leaves the house on S Street, supported on the right side by his cane (he called it his third leg) and on the left side by Isaac Scott, who with his wife, Mary, helped care for the Wilsons in retirement. Wilson died in his bedroom on the third floor of the house on February 3, 1924. Mrs. Wilson lived on in the house for almost 38 years afterward, dying there on December 28, 1961 — the 105th anniversary of Wilson's birth. (Library of Congress)

been, he became increasingly depressed as he discovered that he had difficulty in recognizing people on the street from his motor car, as well as great difficulty in reading, and that new glasses did not remedy the difficulty. This was a sign of progressive arteriosclerosis.

On January 31, 1924, there came a sudden turn for the worse. His stomach ceased to function, and the kidneys were involved. . . . He said to me in one of his last articulate sentences, "The machinery is worn out."[5]

The word got out, and crowds gathered in front of the house. On the morning of February 2, 1924, Grayson came out and said, "His life is slowly ebbing away. He is a fighting man and he is making a game fight, but I think he realizes his fight is over. He is as brave as a man could be. It breaks one all up to see the fight he is making."[6] Grayson came out several more times to say that the ex-president was sinking. Late the next morning, the doctor came out for the last time. "Mr. Wilson died at eleven-fifteen this morning," he said. "His heart action became feebler and feebler and the heart muscle was so fatigued that it refused to act any longer. The end came peacefully."[7]

The nation mourned. On the day of the funerals—a private one in the house on S Street and a public one at the National Cathedral—church bells tolled and guns of the army and navy fired in salute to the fallen leader. An army bugler sounded taps as the casket sank into a vault at the cathedral.

Edith Wilson lived on to a great age in the house on S Street, keeping it just as it was when she and the ex-president moved into it. When she died in 1961, at the age of 89, the house passed at her request to the National Trust for Historic Preservation, which keeps it open for guided tours. She had spent much of her time in the nearly 38 years since Wilson's death doing all she could to burnish his reputation; on the day she died, which happened to be the 105th anniversary of his birth, she was scheduled to attend the dedication of the Woodrow Wilson Bridge over the Potomac River in Washington. Some years before her death, Wilson's body had been moved from the vault at the National Cathedral to a niche in the cathedral wall, and she was buried there with him.

The reputation that she sought to burnish shines brightly now without help. Wilson is remembered as an innovative and bold leader, who greatly strengthened the role of the president as head of his party, shepherd of his legislative program in Congress and molder of public opinion.

Above all, he is remembered for his vision of an international peacekeeping body. Although he lost his fight to take the United States into the League of Nations, the idea endured. The League of Nations came into being and functioned in the years between the two world wars. After World War II, which Wilson had predicted as resulting from the flawed settlement of World War I, the United Nations took the League's place—with the United States as a member—and the world has seen no worldwide war since that time.

Notes

1. Arthur Walworth, *Woodrow Wilson* (New York: W. W. Norton and Company, 1978), vol. 2, p. 412.
2. Gene Smith, *When the Cheering Stopped* (New York: William Morrow and Company, 1964), p.208.
3. Smith, *When the Cheering Stopped*, p. 231.
4. *The New York Times*, November 12, 1923, p. 1.
5. Cary T. Grayson, *Woodrow Wilson, An Intimate Memoir*, (New York: Holt, Rinehart and Winston, 1960), pp. 138–139.
6. *The New York Times,* February 3, 1924, p. 1.
7. *The New York Times*, February 4, 1924, p. 1.

CHRONOLOGY

1856	Thomas Woodrow Wilson born in Staunton, Va., on December 28
1858	Family moves to Augusta, Ga.
1870	Family moves to Columbia, S.C.
1873	Wilson enters Davidson College
1874	Leaves Davidson; family moves to Wilmington, N.C.
1875	Wilson enters College of New Jersey (later named Princeton University)
1879	Graduates from college; enters University of Virginia law school
1880	Leaves law school, finishes law studies at home
1882	Opens law practice in Atlanta with Edward I. Renick as partner
1883	Begins graduate study at the Johns Hopkins University with the aim of turning to teaching
1885	Wilson's *Congressional Government* published; he marries Ellen Axson and joins the faculty at Bryn Mawr College
1888	Leaves Bryn Mawr and becomes professor at Wesleyan University
1890	Leaves Wesleyan, named professor of jurisprudence and political economy at Princeton

1902	Elected president of Princeton
1910	Elected governor of New Jersey
1912	Elected president of the United States
1914	Ellen Wilson dies
1915	Wilson marries Edith Bolling Galt
1916	Reelected president
1917	Asks Congress for war declaration on April 2
1918	Sets forth Fourteen Points as basis for peace settlement
1918	Armistice ends World War I on November 11; Wilson goes to Paris for peace conference
1919	Peace treaty signed at Versailles on June 28
1919	Wilson begins cross-country trip to rouse support for League of Nations on September 3
1919	Falters speaking at Pueblo, Colorado, on September 25; remainder of trip canceled the next day
1919	Wilson suffers major stroke on October 2, paralyzing his left side and impairing his vision
1921	Term as president ends on March 4
1924	Wilson dies on February 3

FURTHER READING

Garraty, John A. *Woodrow Wilson*. Westport, Conn.: Greenwood Press, 1977. A good read because Garraty is free with his opinions, which the reader can compare with his or her own.

Grayson, Cary T. *Woodrow Wilson: An Intimate Memoir*. New York: Holt, Rinehart and Winston, 1960. Full of splendid insights and anecdotes arising from Grayson's close relationship with Wilson as his physician from 1913 on.

Heckscher, August. *Woodrow Wilson*. New York: Charles Scribner's Sons, 1991. A modern work, benefiting from recently published Wilson papers.

Hoover, Irwin Hood. *Forty-two Years in the White House*. Boston: Houghton Mifflin Company, 1934. Rich in tales of life in the Wilson White House as seen by the longtime chief usher there.

Link, Arthur S. *Wilson* (5 vols.). Princeton, N.J.: Princeton University Press, 1947–1965. A majestic work, filled with details of Wilson's career, but the five volumes take that career up only to the time of America's entry into World War I in 1917.

Link, Arthur S. *Woodrow Wilson: A Brief Biography*. Cleveland and New York: The World Publishing Company, 1963. Here Link ably describes Wilson's entire career in only 180 pages.

Link, Arthur S., ed. *Woodrow Wilson: A Profile*. New York: Hill and Wang, 1968. The profile is sketched by 17 people who knew Wilson well at various stages of his life or have studied his career closely.

McAdoo, Eleanor Wilson. *The Woodrow Wilsons*. New York: Macmillan, 1937. The author is Wilson's third daughter and youngest child, and she supplies anecdotes about the family's life that could not be found elsewhere.

Smith, Gene. *When the Cheering Stopped*. New York: William Morrow and Company, 1964. A moving account of Wilson's last years.

Starling, Edmund W. *Starling of the White House*. New York: Simon and Schuster, 1946. Starling was a Secret Service agent assigned to the White House who often accompanied Wilson in the president's public appearances and greatly admired him.

Walworth, Arthur. *Woodrow Wilson* (third edition, 2 vols.). New York: W. W. Norton and Company, Inc., 1978. A thorough but rather worshipful account that won the Pulitzer Prize for biography.

Weinstein, Edwin A. *Woodrow Wilson: A Medical and Psychological Biography*. Princeton, N.J.: Princeton University Press, 1981. Weinstein, a psychiatrist, has studied Wilson's medical records and offers many opinions about his subject's career and health.

Wilson, Edith Bolling. *My Memoir*. Indianapolis and New York: The Bobbs-Merrill Company, 1939. Wilson's second wife is even more worshipful than Walworth, but she supplies many anecdotes that no one else could offer.

INDEX

Italic numbers indicate illustrations.